ITALIAN DISHES

An abundance of delicious recipes, using the finest of wholefood ingredients, which have established Italian cuisine as among the best in the world.

By the same author
PASTA DISHES
PIZZAS AND PANCAKES
QUICHES AND FLANS
THE RAW FOOD WAY TO HEALTH
SIMPLE AND SPEEDY WHOLEFOOD COOKING
A VEGETARIAN IN THE FAMILY
THE WHOLEFOOD LUNCH BOX
THE WHOLEFOOD SWEETS BOOK

In the same series
BAKING BETTER BREADS
THE BROWN RICE COOKBOOK
CAKES, SCONES AND BISCUITS
INDIAN CURRIES
THE MAGIC OF TOFU
PIES, BAKES AND CASSEROLES
SALADS
VEGETARIAN DINNER PARTIES

ITALIAN DISHES

by

JANET HUNT

Illustrated by Clive Birch

A THORSONS WHOLEFOOD COOKBOOK

THORSONS PUBLISHERS LIMITED
Wellingborough, Northamptonshire

First published 1983

British Library Cataloguing in Publication Data

Hunt, Janet
Italian Dishes
1. Cooking, Italian
I. Title
641.5945 TX723

ISBN 0-7225-0815-8

Printed in Great Britain by
Richard Clay (The Chaucer Press) Ltd,
Bungay, Suffolk

With thanks to the many people
who helped me write this book,
especially Mary, for filling me in
on the details, and Veronica for
checking (and correcting!) my Italian.

CONTENTS

Wholefoods, quite simply, are foods in their natural state — nothing added, nothing taken away. In this age of mass-production foods, wholefoods are not always easy to obtain. But as nutritionists and doctors become increasingly convinced of their value in building and maintaining health, so their availability is fast improving.

Include as many natural, unadulterated foods as you can in your day to day pattern, and discover not just exciting new tastes and a fresh approach to mealtimes, but better health too.

INTRODUCTION

We have all heard tales of the gargantuan banquets that were held during the days of the Roman Empire, huge tables laden with such 'delicacies' as stewed flamingo tongue, swans decorated with their own plumage, whole sheep stuffed with birds, boar stuffed with oysters, hedgehogs, puppies — and dormice rolled in honey and poppy seeds for those with a sweet tooth. Emperor Maximinus, it was said, could eat 40 lb of meat a day, with 40 quarts of wine to wash it down. Such stories, based on the truth if not completely accurate, have tended to overshadow an important fact — the ancient Romans were mostly vegetarians. Certainly the affluent few gorged themselves at feasts of this kind, but they were a very small minority. The majority of people existed on a more frugal diet of vegetables, fruits, nuts and grains, with the occasional addition of some cottage cheese made from ewe's milk.

It was also only for a limited period that the 'lucky' few dined so ostentatiously. When the Roman Empire fell, so, for many years, did any interest in cookery. It was not until the Renaissance that food again became a popular way of impressing others with your wealth. This time, however, serving meat in such sickening amounts was no longer the practice. Instead, novelty was what counted. Using new cookery techniques, new combinations of ingredients, discovering entirely new tastes — these were what made your dinner a success. It was then that the long-lived Italian fondness for vegetables was born. Pasta became popular, and was made not just in private homes, but in factories too — commercial production actually began in Naples during the Renaissance. In Sicily and the south, the highly specialized art of making ice-cream and other sweetmeats — an art brought over by the Arabs — was being perfected. Vegetables, pasta and ice-cream are still very important to Italian cuisine.

Although many such foods are found throughout Italy, other ingredients and cooking methods are specific only to a particular area. This is partly because, until as recently as 1861, Italy was divided into different states, each one with different geographic situation, traditions and lifestyle. Although now united under one government, many of those differences still exist. In the far north, for example, the food is solid and filling to help combat the harsh winters. White truffles, found virtually nowhere else, are a speciality of Piedmontese cooking.

Liguria, a long thin state that stretches along the coast, relies heavily on fish for its protein. Bologna, surrounded by the most fertile land in the country, is famous for its rich dishes laced generously with butter, cream and cheese, whereas in Tuscany the food is plain and wholesome, true peasant-style fare. In Abruzzi, where the land is more barren, simple ingredients are made interesting by the addition of strongly flavoured peppers. And Neopolitan cookery, as everyone knows, is abundant in tomatoes, garlic, onions and olive oil — the ingredients that grow so well in that particular climate and soil.

Even the islands vary considerably — though logically, when you think about it. Sardinia has poor soil, and because of its position has had few influences from the outside world. There, the diet is much as it has always been, with protein coming from whatever the hunter can catch — wild boar, even bear, and small birds such as quail and thrushes. Sicily, despite its mountains, has good growing soil and a long growing season. The Sicilians eat little meat, enjoying instead excellent crops of vegetables, fruit, and wheat, which they make into pasta. And as most invaders from the south seemed to have stopped off en route at Sicily, the ways in which these ingredients are served tend to be more exotic than elsewhere in Italy — couscous, for example, being a favourite dish with the locals.

If ingredients and cooking methods differ considerably throughout Italy, one thing that remains constant is the Italian attitude to food. Mealtimes are when the family come together, and as families are still an important part of life in Italy, so are mealtimes. Mostly it is the woman of the family who cooks, a task in which she takes both pride and pleasure. Catering very often for large numbers of people at both the midday as well as the evening meal, the housewife must spend most of her day either shopping for food or preparing it. Because she sees this not as an intrusion on her life, but possibly the most important aspect of it, the room in which she spends so much time must be spacious, well-equipped, pleasant in atmosphere and outlook. Surprisingly, most kitchens, even in the poorer south, live up to these standards. The Italian man may not think much about Women's Lib, but he loves his wife as well as his food. He would feel he was failing if he didn't give her the best kitchen he could afford, and money spent on that room — or on food to be prepared in it — is never considered wasted. It is interesting to note that some of today's most elegant and efficient kitchen furniture and fittings are designed by Italians.

The tradition of Italian cookery goes back literally thousands of years, during which time it has evolved to become one of the most popular cuisines in the world. It is a shame, then, that this last century has seen one major change that could well ruin it completely — the widespread acceptance of refined foods, tinned foods, artificially grown foods. It was not so long ago that bread, pizzas and pastas were made with wholegrains; that vegetables and fruits grew prolifically with no encouragement from man; that eggs, nuts, olives and wild mushrooms could be found no further away than the back yard.

Today, as elsewhere in the world, Italians rely on processed foods, refined grains and sugar, on vegetable and fruit crops pushed to their limits by chemical fertilizers. It may help the country's economy, but does little for the quality of its food, nor for the livelihoods of the many peasants and village people who just cannot compete. Grocers' stores now sell frozen peas alongside the locally-grown fresh ones, tinned fruit salad alongside fat peaches and shiny cherries, processed cheese as well as fresh Ricotta made by the grocer's daughter. And because his customers are all too familiar with the peas, the fresh fruit, the Ricotta, it is the processed foods they consider new and desirable, even though they are usually more expensive.

To be fair, refined foods reached Italy some time after they arrived here. In Britain and America there is now a strong, and fast becoming established, swing back to wholefoods, a growing awareness that simple, unadulterated foods taste better as well as offering more nutrients. This return to old-fashioned foods has not gone unnoticed in Italy. Thinking people are already becoming conscious of the mistake they are making, and shops are beginning to cater for their desire to put the mistake right. And powerful trends grow from such small beginnings.

The recipes in this book are traditional in two senses. Mostly they are recipes that have been passed from mother to daughter, and though each may make some slight adaptations of her own, grandma would no doubt still recognize the results. Secondly, they are based on wholefoods — the ingredients, that is, that grandma would probably have used in the first place. Try the recipes as they are given, and hopefully you will discover a whole new pleasure in Italian food, as well as better health, a slimmer figure, and lots of vitality.

Buon appetito!

Ingredients You Will Need

Many of the ingredients you will need to cook the recipes in this book are probably to be found ready waiting in your fridge or cupboard. If, however, you intend to cook Italian food on a regular basis, it is worth stocking up with the things you would expect to find in an Italian kitchen — all the things, in fact, that give simple dishes a very different character. These, then, are the items you should look out for:

Fresh vegetables, salads and fruit: Always the most important items if you want to create interesting dishes — and a healthy family. Buy them in small quantities, preferably in season, better still locally grown. The Italian housewife goes to her local market most mornings to get the ingredients she will need that day.

Pulses: The most widely used pulses in Italy are canellini, borlotti and kidney beans; chick peas (garbanzo beans); whole lentils, both green and brown. Although these are best bought in their dry state, and soaked overnight before cooking, it is a good idea to keep a few tins handy for emergency use.

Nuts: Quite understandably, those that grow in Italy are the ones that are most widely and frequently used. Buy small amounts of almonds, hazelnuts and pine nuts so you use them whilst they are fresh. Chestnuts are also very useful. If they are out of season, use the dried or tinned varieties instead.

Cheeses: Every area produces its own cheeses, all of them unique, and most of them consumed by local people, as they do not travel well. There are, however, a number of Italian cheeses now available virtually everywhere. The best known is Parmesan, a hard, pungent cheese made from cow's milk, and used principally for grating (though when young, it can be eaten like any other cheese, and has a much milder flavour). Parmesan is best bought in a lump, or at least freshly grated, as the pre-packed variety has usually lost much of its flavour before it even reaches you. Mozzarella, a mild, semi-soft cheese, is mostly used for cooking. It was originally made from buffalo's milk — and still is in parts of the south — but most of the Mozzarella on sale today is made from cow's milk. If you cannot find it, Bel Paese makes a good substitute. Ricotta is a versatile soft, white cheese that can be used in savoury and sweet dishes. It is becoming more widely available out of Italy, but if you have difficulty buying it, use cottage cheese mashed with a few spoonsful of cream, or curd cheese instead. Gorgonzola, a strong, blue cheese, and Dolcelatte, which is a blend of Gorgonzola and cream cheese, are now both sold in delicatessens across the country. Harder Italian cheeses are more difficult to find, however. Try using better known cheeses such as Cheddar and Edam to replace them if necessary.

Eggs: The Italians use eggs to add richness and protein to many of their dishes. Try to buy free-range whenever possible.

Butter and margarine: The northern Italians have always preferred butter to anything else — the undyed, unsalted variety, that is. They tend to use it on their vegetables and pasta rather than on bread, and in strictly controlled amounts. However, vegetable margarines are becoming better known and increasingly popular in cooking.

Vegetable oils: As olives grow so well in Italy, it is natural that the locals should use olive oil more than any other vegetable oil. (In the south they use it as the northerners would use butter.) Olive oil comes in a variety of colours and textures, each ideal for a different purpose. Buy the best quality you can afford (preferably cold pressed), and use it sparingly. When slow frying, use half olive oil, half butter — the oil prevents the butter from burning. Other vegetable oils are, however, finding their way into Italian kitchens, especially for use when cooking. Corn and sunflower are good ones to look out for.

When following the recipes in this book, use whichever kind of oil you prefer, although when the ingredients list specifies olive oil, it is because its unique flavour will make the dish taste more authentic.

Vinegar: The Italians use best quality white or red wine vinegars.

Tomatoes: Fresh ones are obviously preferable from a nutritional point of view, but tinned tomatoes and *purées* (pastes) from Italy do have a different flavour. Besides, it is handy to have some in the cupboard for when you run out of fresh ones.

Capers: The easiest way ever to give a dish a Mediterranean character. Buy them in jars or tins.

Vegetable stock cubes: You would be unlikely to find these in an Italian cupboard — but they are invaluable for putting together a soup, or adding flavour to a risotto, when you have no freshly made stock on hand.

Sugar: Few Italians use raw brown sugar, but then they do not consume as much as we British do either! For your health's sake, use raw cane sugar in all your cooking — there are now some very pale varieties available so your baking will look virtually the same as that made with white sugar, if that is what you want.

Honey: Frequently used out of the cities, where it is made by locals for use by locals. A good healthy ingredient to incorporate in your cooking.

Flour: Wholemeal flour — *farina integrale* — is now much more widely used in Italy, especially for baking bread. Most of it, however, has the wheatgerm removed, presumably to give it a longer shelf life. You can use 100% wholemeal flour in all the recipes given in this book, but if you want your food to *look* more like the real thing, use 81% wholemeal instead.

Pasta: Although most of the wholemeal pasta we get in this country is imported from Italy, wholemeal pasta is not very popular with Italians. Serve whichever kind you and your family prefer — but remember that you are only getting half the goodness if you choose white.

Brown rice: Also imported from Italy, and not widely used there, although it is far more popular now than it used to be despite the fact that it costs considerably more than white rice.

Wine: As the Italians make more wine than anyone else in the world, it is understandable that they like to use it in their cooking — and have been doing so since Roman times, in fact. If you want to follow their example, be careful not to use the really cheap and nasty kind, or you'll end up with a nasty taste in your mouth.

Herbs: These are much used in Italian cookery, usually fresh rather than dried. If possible, grow your own. Varieties that are used most often are basil, oregano, parsley (the Italian *prezzemole* is flat leaved and more pungent than the kind we get here), marjoram, rosemary, bay leaves. Borage, rarely used in English cookery, is often used in Italy, not just to add flavour, but as a stuffing for ravioli, or as fritters. Fennel leaves are another favourite — try adding them to mayonnaise.

Garlic: Although it features often in Italian dishes, the flavour should not be overpowering. Judge the quantities to use for yourself, remembering the strength of the garlic depends on its age, variety and size. The purple-skinned ones tend to be sweeter.

Spices: Also used frequently, especially in sweet dishes, and the Italian cook prefers them freshly ground. Stock up with nutmeg, cinnamon, coriander, cloves. Vanilla pods are often used — keep one or two in a jar of sugar for use when making sweet pastry. Aniseed and fennel are popular too. Saffron is used to flavour soups and *gnocchi* as well as the famous *risotto alla milanese*. Made from the pistils of the autumn-flowering crocus (of which there are only three for each flower) it is understandably expensive. But it does make such a difference to a special dish.

Soya 'bacon' bits: Again, you would not expect to find these in an Italian store cupboard. But it is amazing how many basically vegetarian dishes are flavoured with a few pieces of bacon! You can, of course, make up for this by adding extra seasoning or herbs — or, if you want your dish to taste as Italian as possible, throw in a few soya 'bacon' bits.

Olives: In Italy they come in a huge range of shapes and sizes, though you may not find such a choice at your local shop. However, they are well worth tracking down, and you need use only a few at a time to make an effect. Buy them, if possible, by weight rather than pre-packed. Store any unused olives in a jar topped up with olive oil.

Seasoning: No self-respecting Italian would use any salt except sea salt, nor any pepper except whole peppercorns, both ground at the table. At one time, however, anchovies were used to salt a dish, as the high tax on salt itself made it a luxury few could afford.

Note: All quantities are for 4 average servings.

1.
SOUPS

Soups are a popular all-year-round first course in Italy, sometimes taking the place of pasta, though they often share the menu. To the question 'What are you putting in the soup?' most Italian housewives answer with another question 'What's in the larder?'. They rarely follow recipes, but ad lib as they go along, using any ingredients that are handy including left-overs, less-than-perfect vegetables, and stock from yesterday's dinner, probably either chicken or vegetable. This way — despite the fact that soup is served most days — it never becomes boring.

The recipes given here are typical of the kind of soups you would eat in either private homes or restaurants in Italy, though the details may vary considerably from region to region. Many of them involve *puréeing* the cooked ingredients to make a smoother, thicker soup. If you do not have a blender, cannot be bothered with using a sieve — or just prefer your soups to have more texture — serve them just as they are. To make the stock a little thicker, in this case, stir in some flour, lentils, rice, or a spoonful of cream or yogurt.

One of the simplest and most delicious soups of all is made by chopping up a wide variety of vegetables, adding them to a well-flavoured vegetable stock with a few herbs, and simmering until the vegetables are just tender. Served with a sprinkling of grated cheese this is a meal in itself, made in no time at all, and nutritious too.

ONION AND WHITE WINE SOUP

Minestra di cipolle al vino bianco

Imperial (Metric)	American
1½ lb (¾ kilo) onions	1½ pounds onions
1½ oz (40g) margarine or butter	3½ tablespoonsful margarine or butter
1 oz (25g) wholemeal flour	¼ cupful wholewheat flour
1¾ pints (900ml) vegetable stock	4½ cupsful vegetable stock
⅓ pint (200ml) white wine	¾ cupful white wine
Seasoning to taste	Seasoning to taste
4 rounds wholemeal bread	4 rounds wholewheat bread
4 oz (100g) grated cheese	1 cupful grated cheese

1. Peel and chop the onions finely. Melt the margarine in a saucepan and *sauté* the onions for 5 minutes, or until they begin to soften.
2. Add the flour, stir well, then pour in the vegetable stock and white wine.
3. Stir the ingredients, cover the saucepan, and cook over a low heat for about 30 minutes. Season generously.
4. Just before serving, put a round of toasted bread in the bottom of four soup bowls. Divide the soup between the bowls, sprinkle with cheese and — if liked — pop them under the grill briefly before taking them to the table. Extra cheese can be passed around in a separate dish.

CREAM OF CELERY SOUP

Crema di sedano

Imperial (Metric)	**American**
1 head of celery	1 head of celery
2 medium leeks	2 medium leeks
2 oz (50g) margarine or butter	5 tablespoonsful margarine or butter
1½ pints (¾ litre) vegetable stock	3¾ cupsful vegetable stock
1 oz (25g) wholemeal flour	¼ cupful wholewheat flour
1 oz (25g) margarine or butter	2½ tablespoonsful margarine or butter
½ pint (¼ litre) milk	1⅓ cupsful milk
2 tablespoonsful cream	2 tablespoonsful cream
Seasoning to taste	Seasoning to taste
Celery leaves to garnish	Celery leaves to garnish

1. Wash, trim and chop the celery and leeks. Melt the margarine in a pan, add the prepared vegetables, and cook for about 5 minutes.
2. Pour on the stock, bring to the boil, cover the pan and simmer gently for 30 minutes or until soft. Remove from heat.
3. When vegetables have cooled sufficiently, *purée* them in a blender, or rub them through a sieve.
4. Meanwhile, make a white sauce by melting the remaining margarine then *sautéeing* the flour. As it begins to colour, add the milk gradually and bring to the boil, stirring continuously, until the sauce thickens.
5. Add the vegetable *purée* and reheat gently. Stir in the cream and season to taste. Serve topped with a sprinkling of chopped celery leaves.

Note: To make this soup even more velvety *and* nutritious, beat an egg yolk into the cream that you add at the last minute — cook for a minute or two, then season and serve.

BROCCOLI AND RICE SOUP

Minestra di broccoli e riso

Imperial (Metric)

1 lb (450g) fresh or frozen broccoli
2 medium onions
1 lb (450g) potatoes
2 pints (1 litre) vegetable stock
2 oz (50g) brown rice
1 oz (25g) margarine or butter
Seasoning to taste
Grated Parmesan cheese to serve (optional)

American

1 pound fresh or frozen broccoli
2 medium onions
1 pound potatoes
5 cupsful vegetable stock
4 tablespoonsful brown rice
2½ tablespoonsful margarine or butter
Seasoning to taste
Grated Parmesan cheese to serve (optional)

1. Trim and wash the broccoli, then break into large florets and put in a saucepan.
2. Peel and slice the onions; peel and cube the potatoes.
3. Add them to the broccoli with the vegetable stock, bring to the boil, cover and simmer for 30 minutes, or until all the vegetables are tender. Cool for a few minutes, then *purée* in a blender or rub through a sieve.
4. Return the mixture to the saucepan and, if very thick, add a drop more vegetable stock.
5. Stir in the margarine and rice, bring to boil again, then simmer covered for about 20 minutes, or until the rice is cooked.
6. Season to taste and serve at once. Parmesan cheese goes well with this soup, though it's delicious and filling eaten just as it is — and, of course, ideal for vegans.

NOODLES IN BROTH

Pasta in brodo al pesto

Imperial (Metric)
2 pints (1 litre) good vegetable stock
2 oz (50g) wholemeal noodles
2 tablespoonsful pesto sauce (see page 101)
Seasoning to taste

American
5 cupsful good vegetable stock
¼ cupful wholewheat noodles
2 tablespoonsful pesto sauce (see page 101)
Seasoning to taste

1. Bring the vegetable stock to the boil in a large pan.
2. Break the pasta into small pieces and sprinkle onto the stock, then cook over a medium heat for just a few minutes, by which time the noodles should be tender and will rise to the surface.
3. Stir in the pesto sauce until dissolved, and season to taste (this may not be necessary if the stock is well flavoured). Serve at once.

VEGETABLE SOUP

Minestrone verde

Imperial (Metric)	American
3 oz (75g) canellini or haricot beans	½ cupful canellini or navy beans
3 tablespoonsful vegetable oil	3 tablespoonsful vegetable oil
2 large tomatoes	2 large tomatoes
2 leeks	2 leeks
1 clove garlic, crushed	1 clove garlic, crushed
1 potato	1 potato
½ small cauliflower	½ small cauliflower
2 pints (1 litre) vegetable stock	5 cupsful vegetable stock
2 oz (50g) wholemeal pasta shells	1 cupful wholewheat pasta shells
Parsley	Parsley
Fresh green herbs	Fresh green herbs
Seasoning to taste	Seasoning to taste
Grated Parmesan cheese to serve	Grated Parmesan cheese to serve

1. Soak the beans overnight, then cook in plenty of water until just tender. (Or use left-overs and save yourself time and effort.)
2. In a large saucepan heat the oil, then add the chopped tomatoes, cleaned chopped leeks and the garlic. Cook until the tomatoes begin to form a sauce.
3. Peel and cube the potato and add it to the pan with the cauliflower, broken into florets, and the vegetable stock. Cook for 10 minutes.
4. Add the pasta shells, beans and a generous handful of chopped parsley and herbs — cook 10 minutes more.
5. Check that all the ingredients are tender and season the soup to taste. Serve very hot, and hand round a dish of cheese for those that want to sprinkle it onto their soup in the traditional way.

Note: This is one of many different versions of the popular *minestrone*, each area having its own. As it is called a *green* soup, add plenty of parsley and herbs. Green beans like flageolets, though not widely used in Italy, will heighten the colourful effect.

SWEETCORN, BEAN AND BARLEY SOUP

Zuppa di mais, fagioli e orzo

Imperial (Metric)

2 tablespoonsful vegetable oil
1-2 cloves garlic, crushed
4 oz (100g) sweetcorn kernels, fresh or frozen
4 oz (100g) borlotti beans, soaked overnight
4 oz (100g) pearl or pot barley, soaked overnight
2 pints (1 litre) vegetable stock
1 large leek
Seasoning to taste
Parsley

American

2 tablespoonsful vegetable oil
1-2 cloves garlic, crushed
½ cupful sweetcorn kernels, fresh or frozen
½ cupful borlotti beans, soaked overnight
½ cupful pearl or pot barley, soaked overnight
5 cupsful vegetable stock
1 large leek
Seasoning to taste
Parsley

1. Heat the oil and fry the garlic gently till it begins to colour.
2. Add the sweetcorn (defrost and drain first if using the frozen kind), plus the drained beans, barley, and the vegetable stock. Bring to the boil, then cook gently for 50 minutes.
3. Clean the leek, chop coarsely, and add to the saucepan, and continue cooking for about 10 minutes more, or until all the ingredients are tender.
4. Just before serving season the soup to taste, and stir in a generous amount of chopped parsley.

LETTUCE SOUP

Minestra di lattuga

An ideal way to use up the tough, outer leaves of less-than-perfect lettuces.

Imperial (Metric)	American
2 oz (50g) margarine or butter	5 tablespoonsful margarine or butter
1 oz (25g) wholemeal flour	1/4 cupful wholewheat flour
2 pints (1 litre) vegetable stock	5 cupsful vegetable stock
2 celery sticks	2 celery sticks
1/2 clove garlic, crushed	1/2 clove garlic, crushed
1 large lettuce or equivalent in outer leaves	1 large lettuce or equivalent in outer leaves
4 oz (100g) brown rice	1/2 cupful brown rice
Seasoning to taste	Seasoning to taste
Chopped mint to garnish	Chopped mint to garnish

1. In a saucepan melt the margarine, sprinkle in the flour, and cook for a minute.
2. Pour in the vegetable stock, add the finely chopped celery and garlic, bring to the boil then cover and simmer for 5 minutes.
3. Clean and chop the lettuce leaves, and add to the soup with the rice. Cover the pan again and cook for 20 minutes or until the rice is tender.
4. Season to taste. Serve garnished with fresh mint.

CHESTNUT SOUP

Zuppa di castagne

Imperial (Metric)	**American**
¾ lb (350g) chestnuts	12 ounces chestnuts
2 oz (50g) margarine or butter	5 tablespoonsful margarine or butter
1 large onion	1 large onion
1 large carrot	1 large carrot
1 stick celery	1 stick celery
2 pints (1 litre) vegetable stock	5 cupsful vegetable stock
Seasoning to taste	Seasoning to taste
Pinch of nutmeg	Pinch of nutmeg

1. Make a cut in the top of each chestnut, then either bake them in a slow oven or boil in a pan of water for about 10 minutes. Cool slightly, then peel off the outer shell and inner skin, and halve the nuts.

2. Melt the margarine and add the peeled and chopped onion and carrot; clean, slice and add the celery. *Sauté* for a few minutes to soften and lightly colour the vegetables.

3. Pour on the stock, return the prepared chestnuts to the pan, and cook for 20-30 minutes, or until all the ingredients are tender.

4. Leave to cool for a few minutes, then liquidize the soup in a blender, or by pushing it through a sieve.

5. Re-heat gently, season, and serve at once. Sprinkle each bowl with a little nutmeg.

SPINACH AND PINE NUT SOUP

Minestra di spinaci ai pinoli

Imperial (Metric)	**American**
1 lb (450g) fresh or frozen spinach	1 pound fresh or frozen spinach
2 oz (50g) margarine or butter	5 tablespoonsful margarine or butter
1 large onion	1 large onion
1 clove garlic, crushed	1 clove garlic, crushed
½ oz (15g) wholemeal flour	2 tablespoonsful wholewheat flour
2 pints (1 litre) vegetable stock	5 cupsful vegetable stock
2 tablespoonsful cream	2 tablespoonsful cream
2 oz (50g) pine nuts	4 tablespoonsful pine nuts
Seasoning to taste	Seasoning to taste
Pinch of nutmeg	Pinch of nutmeg

1. Wash, shred, and steam or boil the spinach in the minimum amount of water until tender. Drain, chop finely, and set aside.
2. Melt the margarine and gently cook the peeled, chopped onion with the crushed garlic for 5 minutes.
3. Sprinkle in the flour and *sauté* briefly, then slowly add the vegetable stock, stirring well. Bring to the boil.
4. Add the chopped spinach and cook a few minutes more.
5. Lower the heat and stir in the cream and nuts — continue cooking another minute but take care the soup does not boil.
6. When ready to serve the soup, season it to taste and add a pinch of nutmeg.

EGG SOUP WITH PASTA

Stracciatella con pasta

Imperial (Metric)
1 oz (25g) wholemeal noodles
2 large eggs
1 oz (25g) wholemeal semolina
2 oz (50g) grated Parmesan cheese
2 pints (1 litre) vegetable stock
1 tablespoonful chopped parsley
Seasoning to taste

American
½ cupful wholewheat noodles
2 large eggs
¼ cupful wholewheat semolina
½ cupful grated Parmesan cheese
5 cupsful vegetable stock
1 tablespoonful chopped parsley
Seasoning to taste

1. Cook the noodles in boiling water for 5 minutes, or until tender. Drain and set aside.
2. Meanwhile, mix together the beaten eggs, semolina, grated cheese, and just a little of the vegetable stock. Flavour with the parsley and seasoning.
3. Bring the rest of the vegetable stock to the boil, add the noodles, then gradually beat in the egg mixture.
4. Lower the heat and simmer the soup for 3-5 minutes, still stirring continually, by which time the egg should set in small flakes. Serve the soup at once.

2.

ANTIPASTI

An alternative to soup or pasta, antipasti can be as exotic or as simple, as light or as filling as you think it should be — and as the rest of the meal dictates.

Vegetables are a popular choice. They can be served raw, alone or in combinations, and often with a dip or sauce. Italians also like to cook them, then serve them cold — a technique that adds variety although it does detract from the vegetables' nutritional value. The same can be said of probably the most popular antipasti, vegetables in vinegar or oil (or both, of course). Pickled or preserved artichoke hearts, cucumbers, green beans, button mushrooms and pimentos are just some of the varieties served regularly. Olives, both black and green, are probably served daily!

Fresh fruit is not often dished up as an antipasto except in the very well known combinations — *melone o ficci con prosciutto*, melon or fresh figs with Parma ham. Vegetarians might like to try combining the fresh fruits and throwing out the ham for a delicious start to a meal!

Hot antipasti are not so widely served, especially in the summer, but an exception is *crostini*, rounds of toasted or fried bread topped with cheese, vegetables or maybe a bean pâté. Miniature pizzas or a slice of flan also make interesting ways to start your meal.

For more antipasti ideas, see the chapter on salads, most of which could be served to start a meal as well as to freshen the palate half way through it.

FRIED CHEESE STARTER

Mozzarella in carrozza

Imperial (Metric)	American
8 small thin slices wholemeal bread	8 small thin slices wholewheat bread
½ lb (225g) Mozzarella cheese	8 ounces Mozzarella cheese
2 eggs	2 eggs
Pinch of salt	Pinch of salt
Oil for frying	Oil for frying
Tomato and lettuce to serve	Tomato and lettuce to serve

1. Trim the crusts from the bread. Divide the cheese into 4 slices and arrange each one between two pieces of bread.
2. Beat the eggs and salt together lightly, then soak the sandwiches in the mixture, turning them over after about 15 minutes, and leaving for a while longer so that all the egg is absorbed. Press the sandwiches together firmly so that they keep their shape.
3. Heat some vegetable oil in a pan, and shallow fry the cheese sandwiches over a moderate heat for a few minutes on each side. The bread should be golden and crisp, the Mozzarella creamy.
4. Drain on paper towels, cut diagonally and serve hot, garnished with a few slices of tomato and a lettuce leaf or two.

CARROT AND CHEESE BALLS

Palline di carote e formaggio

Imperial (Metric)
½ lb (225g) cream cheese
3 large carrots, finely grated
½ small onion or herbs
Seasoning to taste
Parsley

American
1 cupful cream cheese
3 large carrots, finely grated
½ small onion or herbs
Seasoning to taste
Parsley

1. Use a wooden spoon to soften the cheese, then mix with the finely grated carrots.
2. Grate the onion and add to the mixture if you like a stronger flavour. For a milder taste, use fresh herbs such as basil and oregano instead of the onion. Season to taste.
3. Form the mixture into small balls and roll them in chopped parsley, then set aside in the cool to firm up before serving.

Note: Although these carrot and cheese balls can be served as a starter, they make an excellent appetizer to go with with a pre-meal *aperitivo*.

FRESH ASPARAGUS

Asparagi al burro e formaggio

One of the simplest ways to start a meal, yet one of the most impressive — especially when asparagus are not in season.

Imperial (Metric)	**American**
1 lb (450g) fresh asparagus	1 pound fresh asparagus
3 oz (75g) butter	⅓ cupful butter
2 oz (50g) grated Parmesan cheese	½ cupful grated Parmesan cheese

1. Use a sharp knife to cut off the ends of the asparagus if they are tough and woody, then trim them so that they are about the same length. Wash well.
2. Tie the asparagus into bundles of 8 or so, using thin string to hold them together at the bottom and just below the heads.
3. Stand them upright in a deep saucepan (or a special asparagus pan) and pour enough boiling water to go at least half-way up the stalks.
4. Cover with a lid of silver foil so that the steam cannot escape, and cook for 10-15 minutes or until tender. Fresh cut asparagus will cook even quicker — shop-bought asparagus may be tougher, and need a longer cooking period.
5. Carefully drain away the water and untie the asparagus. Arrange it on a long serving dish with the heads together.
6. Melt the butter and pour it evenly over the asparagus, then sprinkle with cheese. Serve at once.

MIXED ANTIPASTO

Antipasto misto

You can use a wide variety of ingredients to make your *antipasto misto* — in fact, the more the better. Arrange them on one large oval dish, or on individual plates, using the range of colours and shapes to make the food look as appetizing as it is flavoursome. Ingredients to include:

Pimentos in oil
Cucumber chunks
Cherry tomatoes with onion rings
Olives, both black and green
Small artichokes in oil
Raw broad beans (Windsor beans)
Raw mushrooms, sliced thinly
Chicory
Rings of red and green pepper
Raw fennel strips
Quartered hard-boiled eggs
Slices of cheeses such as Mozzarella, Provolone, Gorgonzola, Gruyère
Cooked chick peas (garbanzo beans) and kidney beans

Put a good salad dressing, some mayonnaise, sea salt and a pepper grinder on the table for everyone to add to their *antipasto misto* as they wish.

SPINACH STUFFED EGGS

Uova sode con spinaci

Imperial (Metric)	**American**
4 large eggs	4 large eggs
2 oz (50g) cream cheese	¼ cupful cream cheese
4 oz (100g) spinach, fresh or frozen	4 ounces spinach, fresh or frozen
2 oz (50g) grated Parmesan cheese	½ cupful grated Parmesan cheese
Top of milk	Top of milk
Grated nutmeg	Grated nutmeg
Seasoning to taste	Seasoning to taste
Chives to garnish	Chives to garnish

1. Hard-boil the eggs and set aside to cool.
2. Mash the cream cheese with a spoon to soften it.
3. Cook the spinach in the minimum amount of water until soft, then drain well and chop.
4. Halve the eggs lengthwise and carefully remove the yolk.
4. In a bowl, mix together the cream cheese, spinach, Parmesan cheese, a little top of the milk, nutmeg, seasoning and egg yolks.
5. When thoroughly combined, and creamy in texture, pile the mixture back into the hollows in the egg whites.
6. Arrange them attractively on a serving dish and sprinkle with fresh chopped chives.

ARTICHOKE HEARTS

Cuori di carciofo al limone

Imperial (Metric)	American
14 oz (400g) tin artichoke hearts*	14 ounce tin artichoke hearts*
3 tablespoonsful lemon juice	3 tablespoonsful lemon juice
3 tablespoonsful olive oil	3 tablespoonsful olive oil
1 clove garlic, crushed	1 clove garlic, crushed
Seasoning to taste	Seasoning to taste
Parsley to garnish	Parsley to garnish

1. Drain the artichoke hearts and set aside to chill.
2. Beat together the lemon juice, oil, crushed garlic and seasoning, and when well blended put the dressing also in a cool place for at least an hour.
3. When ready to serve the dish, arrange the artichoke hearts on four small plates, and spoon some of the dressing over each. Sprinkle with finely chopped parsley.

*This antipasto is prepared quickly and easily from tinned artichokes but these are obviously less nutritious and — more often than not — rather tasteless. If you can obtain fresh artichokes at a reasonable price, you will need about sixteen to make four servings. Soak them, for about 30 minutes in cold water, then use a sharp knife to cut off the stem and outer leaves. Trim the tips from the leaves (scissors make this job easier), then carefully scoop or pull out the choke, the hairy centre of the artichoke. Cook in boiling salted water for about 30 minutes, or until tender, then leave upside down to drain as they cool.

Artichoke hearts cooked in this way can also be served cold with mayonnaise instead of the lemon-oil dressing given above.

PICKLED COURGETTES

Zucchini sott' aceto con olio

Imperial (Metric)
4 medium courgettes
4 tablespoonsful olive oil
1 clove garlic
Approx. ¼ pint (150ml) wine vinegar
1 teaspoonful oregano
Seasoning to taste

American
4 medium zucchini
⅓ cupful olive oil
1 clove garlic
Approx. ⅔ cupful wine vinegar
1 teaspoonful oregano
Seasoning to taste

1. Wash, trim, and slice the courgettes (zucchini). Heat half the oil in a pan and *sauté* them for a few minutes until they are lightly browned on both sides. Remove from the pan and drain.
2. In a screwtop jar combine the courgettes (zucchini), quartered garlic clove, remaining oil, and enough wine vinegar to bring the liquid over the top of the vegetables. Flavour with oregano and seasoning, and shake the jar gently so that all the ingredients are well blended.
3. Leave in a cold place, preferably overnight, before serving.

AUBERGINE TOASTS

Crostini di melanzane

Crostini are a very popular starter, and can be served with a wide variety of toppings.

Imperial (Metric)	American
1½ lb (¾ kilo) aubergines	1½ pounds eggplants
1 clove garlic, crushed	1 clove garlic, crushed
Juice of 1 lemon	Juice of 1 lemon
Parsley	Parsley
Marjoram	Marjoram
Approx. 1-2 tablespoonsful vegetable oil	Approx. 1-2 tablespoonsful vegetable oil
Seasoning to taste	Seasoning to taste
4 slices or 8 small rounds wholemeal bread	4 slices or 8 small rounds wholewheat bread
3 hard-boiled eggs	3 hard-boiled eggs
Extra parsley for garnish	Extra parsley for garnish

1. Clean the aubergines (eggplants) and place in a medium oven. Cook, turning them occasionally, for about an hour, or until tender.
2. When cool enough to handle, remove the peel and mash the flesh to a smooth *purée*.
3. Add the garlic, lemon juice, and enough finely chopped parsley and marjoram to both flavour and colour the aubergine (eggplant) mixture.
4. Then gradually pour in the oil, blending well, until the *purée* is creamy in texture. Season to taste.
5. Toast the bread and cool slightly, then pile some of the mixture onto each piece.
6. Top with a slice or two of the egg, and arrange on a serving plate. Garnish with the parsley.

Note: Vegans might like to replace the egg with coarsely chopped chick peas (garbanzo beans) for protein.

GREEN BEANS WITH YOGURT

Fagiolini con yogurt

Imperial (Metric)	**American**
1½ lb (¾ kilo) French beans	1½ pounds snap beans
Parsley	Parsley
Dill	Dill
1 spring onion	1 scallion
1 teaspoonful fennel seeds	1 teaspoonful fennel seeds
¼ pint (150ml) plain yogurt	⅔ cupful plain yogurt
Seasoning to taste	Seasoning to taste
Soya 'bacon' bits (optional)	Soy 'Baco-Bits' (optional)

1. Top and tail the beans, and steam or boil them for about 10 minutes, or until cooked but still crisp. Drain, then rinse with cold water, and put into a bowl.

2. Chop the parsley, dill and onion coarsely, and mix with the beans together with the fennel seed. If possible, let the mixture stand for a short while for the flavours to mingle, but not necessarily in a refrigerator.

3. Serve topped with the yogurt, which can be mixed into the other ingredients at the table. Italians frequently serve fried bacon pieces with French beans — if you like, follow their example using soya 'bacon' bits to make a crisp, salty contrast to the delicately flavoured beans and yogurt.

PIQUANT FENNEL

Finocchi piccanti

Imperial (Metric)	**American**
3 fennel bulbs	3 fennel bulbs
2 oz (50g) butter	4 tablespoonsful butter
Juice of 1 lemon	Juice of 1 lemon
1 teaspoonful thyme	1 teaspoonful thyme
Seasoning to taste	Seasoning to taste
1 tablespoonful capers	1 tablespoonful capers
12 black olives	12 black olives
Fennel leaves to garnish	Fennel leaves to garnish

1. Trim, wash and dry the fennel bulbs, then cut them lengthwise into ¼ in. (6mm) slices.
2. In a large pan melt the butter, and cook the fennel for a few minutes, turning it once.
3. Add a drop of water, the lemon juice, thyme and seasoning, and cover the pan. Continue cooking gently for about 10 minutes, or until the fennel is soft.
4. Remove the lid and cook for just a little longer on a higher heat.
5. When ready to serve the fennel, transfer it to a large decorative dish, spoon the sauce over it, then sprinkle with the capers and olives. The feathery leaves of the fennel make an unusual garnish. Serve hot.

3.

PIZZAS, PANCAKES AND PIES

Pizzas are probably Italy's best known export. Though eaten throughout Italy now, they originated in the south, and when the poverty-stricken Neapolitans went overseas to find their fortunes, they took their pizza recipe with them. (In many cases, this unique but simple food actually made their fortunes for them!)

Nowadays most people have tasted pizza of one kind or another, usually eating it as a snack or light meal. In Italy it is eaten in the same way — though the pizza itself is invariably a far cry from the fast-food pre-frozen version served up in most of the world's big cities. Why the difference should exist is hard to explain. It could be the flour or the water, the way the dough is kneaded, or that the pizza is cooked in a traditional (and very hot) oven. Once you have tasted it you will find the other kind dull — which is a good reason for making your own. Use wholemeal flour, to improve the flavour as well as the food content, then be adventurous with the toppings and generous with the amounts. For speed and convenience, you can always make up more than you need, and freeze the surplus ones.

Pancakes and pies are not such an old-established Italian food, though their popularity is growing fast, especially as a snack food. In Italy you won't find a huge variety of fillings to choose from — the ones given here cover most of them, excepting those that contain meat. However, as is so often the way with Italian cookery, the ingredients are picked at their freshest, blended with care and flavoured with imagination. You can always, of course, go on and make your own adaptations, using the ideas given here as a starting point.

DEEP-FRIED CHEESE PASTIES

Calzoni

A classic Neapolitan recipe, this one.

Imperial (Metric)	**American**
½ lb (225g) pizza dough (pages 42 and 44)	8 ounces pizza dough (pages 42 and 44)
½ lb (225g) Mozzarella cheese	8 ounces Mozzarella cheese
1-2 tablespoonsful olive oil	1-2 tablespoonsful olive oil
Seasoning to taste	Seasoning to taste
Olive oil for deep frying	Olive oil for deep frying

1. Make the dough in the way described in pizza recipes. When well risen, break into half and roll out as thinly as possible. Cut into 8 circles with a large cup or a cutter.
2. Divide the Mozzarella between the dough circles, placing it carefully on one side. Sprinkle lightly with a drop of oil, then season well.
3. Fold the remaining half of the dough over the cheese to make a half-moon shaped pasty, dampen and press down the edges firmly.
4. Drop the pasties a couple at a time into very hot olive oil, and cook for a few minutes so that the outsides are golden and crisp, whilst the cheese inside is soft and creamy. Drain well and serve hot.

Note: Calzone can also be arranged on a lightly greased baking sheet, and cooked in the oven at 400°F/200°C (Gas Mark 6) for 15-20 minutes.

HOME-STYLE PIZZA

Pizza alla casalinga

Dough:

Imperial (Metric)	American
1/4 oz (7g) dried yeast	1/2 teaspoonful dried yeast
Lukewarm water	Lukewarm water
1/2 lb (225g) plain wholemeal flour	2 cupsful plain wholewheat flour
Pinch of salt	Pinch of salt
2 tablespoonsful vegetable oil	2 tablespoonsful vegetable oil

Topping:

Imperial (Metric)	American
1 lb (450g) tomatoes	1 pound tomatoes
6 oz (175g) Mozzarella cheese	6 ounces Mozzarella cheese
2 tablespoonsful vegetable oil	2 tablespoonsful vegetable oil
2 oz (50g) grated Parmesan cheese	1/2 cupful grated Parmesan cheese
Seasoning to taste	Seasoning to taste
2 teaspoonsful oregano	2 teaspoonsful oregano
4 oz (100g) mushrooms	2 cupsful mushrooms
12 black olives	12 black olives

1. Dissolve the yeast in a drop of warm water, and set aside until the mixture begins to bubble.
2. Sift together the flour and salt.
3. Stir the oil into the yeast mixture, then add this to the flour with enough warm water to make a firm but pliable dough. Knead this on a floured board for a few minutes.
4. Place in a bowl, cover with a damp cloth, and leave in a warm, draught-free spot for 30 minutes to an hour, or until well risen.
5. Knead the dough again briefly, then divide into two pieces, shape them into balls, and flatten with a rolling pin to make two large circles.

6. Place these on lightly greased baking sheets and cover with the chopped tomatoes.
7. Slice the Mozzarella and divide the pieces between the two pizzas, arranging them on top of the tomatoes.
8. Sprinkle a little of the oil over each of them, then Parmesan cheese, seasoning and oregano.
9. Slice the mushrooms (unless you are using button mushrooms which look especially attractive as a topping), and arrange them on top of the pizzas together with the olives. Sprinkle the remaining oil over the mushrooms to prevent them getting too dry.
10. Bake at 400°F/200°C (Gas Mark 6) for 25-30 minutes, or until the crust is crisp. Serve at once cut into wedges, or as two hearty individual pizzas.

SMALL ONION PIZZAS

Pizzette con cipolle

Serve as a starter, or at a buffet party. They are also delicious eaten cold at a picnic.

Dough:

Imperial (Metric)	American
¼ oz (7g) dried yeast	½ tablespoonful dried yeast
Lukewarm water	Lukewarm water
6 oz (175g) plain wholemeal flour	1½ cupsful plain wholewheat flour
Pinch of salt	Pinch of salt
2 tablespoonsful vegetable oil	2 tablespoonsful vegetable oil
1 egg	1 egg

Topping:

Imperial (Metric)	American
1 large green pepper	1 large green pepper
1 lb (450g) onions	1 pound onions
3 tablespoonsful vegetable oil	3 tablespoonsful vegetable oil
½ oz (15g) raw cane sugar	1 tablespoonful raw cane sugar
4 oz (100g) grated Emmenthal, or other hard cheese	1 cupful grated Emmenthal, or other hard cheese
Seasoning to taste	Seasoning to taste

1. Dissolve the yeast in a drop of the water, then set aside in a warm spot until it bubbles.
2. Sift together the flour and salt.
3. Add the oil to the yeast mixture, pour this into the flour, and mix well, adding more warm water and the beaten egg to make a smooth, pliable dough.
3. Knead it for a short while, then place in a bowl, cover with a damp teacloth, and leave in a warm draught-free spot to rise.

4. Finely slice the pepper and onions, and fry them gently in the vegetable oil for 10 minutes, or until beginning to soften. Remove from the heat and stir in the sugar, most of the grated cheese and the seasoning.

5. Roll out the pizza dough and cut into 8 rounds about 3½ in. (9cm) across with a cutter or large cup.

6. Arrange these on lightly greased baking sheets and top each one with some of the onion and cheese mixture.

7. Leave them in a warm spot for 30 minutes more, then bake at 400°F/200°C (Gas Mark 6) for about 15 minutes, or until the dough is cooked, adding the rest of the grated cheese after 10 minutes. Serve hot or cold.

Note: Vegans can serve these *pizzettes* by using the dough recipe given for *pizza alla casalinga* (page 42), and by mixing peanut butter instead of cheese with the onions. Not very Italian — but delicious.

MUSHROOM CREPES

Crepes ai funghi

Batter:

Imperial (Metric)	American
4 oz (100g) plain wholemeal flour	1 cupful plain wholewheat flour
Pinch of salt	Pinch of salt
2 large eggs	2 large eggs
½ pint (275ml) milk	1¼ cupsful milk

Filling:

Imperial (Metric)	American
¾ lb (350g) mushrooms	¾ pound mushrooms
2 oz (50g) margarine or butter	5 tablespoonsful margarine or butter
Good squeeze lemon juice	Good squeeze lemon juice
2 tablespoonsful cream	2 tablespoonsful cream

Sauce:

Imperial (Metric)	American
2 oz (50g) margarine or butter	5 tablespoonsful margarine or butter
2 oz (50g) wholemeal flour	½ cupful wholewheat flour
1 pint (550ml) milk	2½ cupsful milk
Pinch of nutmeg	Pinch of nutmeg
Seasoning to taste	Seasoning to taste
4 oz (100g) grated Provolone, or other hard cheese	1 cupful grated Provolone, or other hard cheese

1. Sieve together the flour and salt, add the lightly beaten eggs, then gradually stir in the milk. Continue beating until the batter is smooth and creamy, then set aside in the fridge.

2. Meanwhile, clean and slice the mushrooms, then cook them gently for a few minutes in the margarine and lemon juice. When just tender stir in the cream, season to taste, and also set this mixture aside.

3. Make a white sauce with the remaining ingredients. Melt the margarine, stir in the flour and *sauté* it for a minute or two. Add the milk and cook, stirring continually, until the sauce thickens. Season and flavour with nutmeg to taste.

4. Beat the batter again, and if too thick add a drop more milk or water.

5. Heat a little oil in a frying pan (skillet) and spoon in a thin coating of the batter, turning the pan so it spreads evenly. Cook gently, and when it begins to colour underneath, toss or turn the pancake with a spatula. Cook the other side very briefly. Keep each pancake warm whilst you use the rest of the batter in the same way.

6. Now divide the mushroom mixture between the pancakes, roll each one up, and arrange them side by side in an ovenproof dish.

7. Cover evenly with the sauce, sprinkle cheese over the top of the dish, and bake at 350°F/180°C (Gas Mark 4) for about 30 minutes, or until golden and bubbly. Serve at once.

PANCAKE PIE

Torta di crepes

Batter:

Imperial (Metric)	American
4 oz (100g) plain wholemeal flour	1 cupful plain wholewheat flour
Pinch of salt	Pinch of salt
1 egg	1 egg
½ pint (275ml) milk	1¼ cupsful milk
Vegetable oil for frying	Vegetable oil for frying

Filling:

Imperial (Metric)	American
¾ lb (350g) spinach, fresh or frozen	¾ pound spinach, fresh or frozen
3 tablespoonsful vegetable oil	3 tablespoonsful vegetable oil
1 clove garlic, crushed	1 clove garlic, crushed
1 small onion	1 small onion
½ lb (225g) Ricotta or curd cheese	1 cupful Ricotta or curd cheese
Seasoning to taste	Seasoning to taste
Tomatoes and parsley to garnish	Tomatoes and parsley to garnish

1. Sift together the flour and salt. Make a well in the centre and add the egg, then gradually beat in the milk so that the batter is thick and creamy, and completely free from lumps. Set aside in a cold place, if possible, for 30 minutes to an hour.
2. Clean, trim and then steam the spinach until just cooked.
3. Heat the oil, add the garlic and cook for a few minutes before adding the chopped onion, and cook them gently together until the onion softens.
4. Drain and coarsely chop the spinach, and stir into the garlic and onion mixture.
5. Whilst the mixture is still hot, add the Ricotta cheese, blend thoroughly, and keep in the warm whilst making the pancakes.

6. Heat a small amount of oil in a frying pan (skillet), making sure the base is evenly covered. Beat the batter lightly again, then spoon in just a little of it, tipping the pan so that it spreads. Cook over a medium heat until it begins to brown, then toss or turn it over with a spatula and cook the second side for a minute or two. Set aside in a warm place whilst you make 3 more pancakes.

7. Lay the first pancake on an ovenproof serving dish, spread a third of the spinach and Ricotta mixture over it, then repeat this twice more. Use the last pancake to top the pile, and press down lightly and evenly.

8. Bake at 325°F/170°C (Gas Mark 3) for 15 minutes, or until heated through. Garnish with tomato slices and parsley, and take straight to the table. Serve cut in wedges.

Note: Any extra pancake batter can be kept in the fridge for a day or two. Or make it up into pancakes and freeze them so that you have the makings of this, and many other recipes, ready to hand when you are hungry and short of time.

CHEESE PANCAKES

Crespelle formaggio

Batter:

Imperial (Metric)	**American**
4 oz (100g) plain wholemeal flour	1 cupful plain wholewheat flour
Pinch of salt	Pinch of salt
2 large eggs	2 large eggs
¼ pint (150ml) milk	⅔ cupful milk
¼ pint (150ml) water	⅔ cupful water
Vegetable oil for frying	Vegetable oil for frying

Filling:

Imperial (Metric)	**American**
2 oz (50g) Mozzarella cheese	2 ounces Mozzarella cheese
2 oz (50g) Provolone cheese	2 ounces Provolone cheese
2 oz (50g) Edam cheese	2 ounces Edam cheese
2 oz (50g) grated Parmesan cheese	2 ounces grated Parmesan cheese
Seasoning to taste	Seasoning to taste

Sauce:

Imperial (Metric)	**American**
3 tablespoonsful vegetable oil	3 tablespoonsful vegetable oil
¾ lb (350g) tomatoes	¾ pound tomatoes
Parsley	Parsley
Seasoning to taste	Seasoning to taste

1. Make up the batter by sifting together the flour and salt, stirring in the beaten eggs, then gradually adding the milk and water to make a smooth, creamy mixture. Set aside in the cool.
2. Cube the first three cheeses, mix well, and stir in the grated Parmesan cheese and seasoning to taste.

3. Heat the oil in a saucepan, add the skinned chopped tomatoes, and cook gently — stirring often — until a thick tomato *purée* forms. Add chopped parsley and seasoning.

4. Heat a very small amount of oil in a clean pan, add a spoonful or two of the prepared batter making sure it is spread over the entire surface of the pan. Cook gently until it begins to brown underneath, then turn the pancake and cook the other side lightly. Use up all the batter in the same way.

5. Wrap the pancakes around some of the cheese combination, and lay them side by side in an ovenproof dish. Pour on the tomato sauce, distributing it evenly. Bake the *crespelle* at 350°F/180°C (Gas Mark 4) for 20-30 minutes, and serve at once.

CABBAGE AND CAULIFLOWER PIE

Torta di cavolo e cavolfiore

Crust:

Imperial (Metric)	American
10 oz (275g) plain wholemeal flour	2½ cupsful plain wholewheat flour
Pinch of salt	Pinch of salt
5 oz (130g) margarine or butter	⅔ cupful margarine or butter
Approx. 3 tablespoonsful cold water	Approx. 3 tablespoonsful cold water

Filling:

Imperial (Metric)	American
½ small cabbage	½ small cabbage
½ small cauliflower	½ small cauliflower
2 oz (50g) margarine or butter	5 tablespoonsful margarine or butter
4 hard-boiled eggs	4 hard-boiled eggs
4 oz (100g) Fontina or Gruyère cheese	4 ounces Fontina or Gruyère cheese
Seasoning to taste	Seasoning to taste

1. Sift the flour and salt together in a bowl, then use your fingertips to rub the margarine into the flour to make a crumb-like mixture.
2. Add enough water to bind the mixture to a soft yet firm dough. Wrap in aluminium foil or clingfilm and chill in the fridge whilst you prepare the filling.
3. Shred the cabbage. Break the cauliflower into florets and steam for 5-10 minutes, then drain.
4. Melt the margarine and gently fry first the cabbage, then the cauliflower until tender, keeping them separate. You may need to use a little more margarine.

5. Divide the dough into two, shape into balls then roll out into circles large enough to cover a medium-sized flan dish. Place one of them in the base of the dish, then add a layer of sliced eggs.

6. Top this with half the cabbage, half the cheese cut into slices, and half the cauliflower. Repeat this process to use up the rest of the ingredients adding seasoning between the layers.

7. Place the second circle of pastry over the top of the dish, press the edges to seal, and use any extra pastry to make a pattern on the top. Prick a couple of times with a fork.

8. Bake at 375°F/190°C (Gas Mark 5) for about 30 minutes, or until the pie crust is cooked and nicely browned. Serve hot.

NOODLE FLAN

Crostata con tagliatelle verdi

This is, of course, usually cooked with meat, but the recipe works well with soya 'meat' or even lentils.

Pastry:

Imperial (Metric)	American
½ lb (225g) plain wholemeal flour	2 cupsful plain wholewheat flour
Pinch of salt	Pinch of salt
4 oz (100g) margarine or butter	½ cupful margarine or butter
Approx. 2 tablespoonsful cold water	Approx. 2 tablespoonsful cold water

Filling:

Imperial (Metric)	American
4 oz (100g) mushrooms	2 cupsful mushrooms
½ oz (15g) margarine or butter	1 tablespoonful margarine or butter
½ lb (225g) home-made green noodles (page 95)	1½ cupsful home-made green noodles (page 95)
2 oz (50g) grated cheese	½ cupful grated cheese
3 oz (75g) soya 'mince meat'	⅓ cupful soy 'mince meat'
1 teaspoonful yeast extract	1 teaspoonful yeast extract
Seasoning to taste	Seasoning to taste

Sauce:

Imperial (Metric)	American
1 oz (25g) margarine or butter	2½ tablespoonsful margarine or butter
½ oz (15g) plain wholemeal flour	2 tablespoonsful plain wholewheat flour
¾ pint (425ml) creamy milk	2 cupsful creamy milk
Pinch of nutmeg	Pinch of nutmeg

Topping:

Imperial (Metric)	American
3 tomatoes	3 tomatoes
2 oz (50g) grated cheese	½ cupful grated cheese

1. Sift the flour into a bowl, stir in the salt, and then rub in the margarine until the mixture resembles fine breadcrumbs.

2. Add cold water and knead well to make a pliable dough. Wrap this in aluminium foil or clingfilm and put into the fridge for 30 minutes.

3. Meanwhile, clean and slice the mushrooms. Melt the margarine and *sauté* them for a few minutes so that they soften. Drain and set aside.

4. Cook the noodles in boiling water for 5-10 minutes or until tender. Drain well and mix with the mushrooms and grated cheese. Set aside again.

5. Cover the soya 'mince meat' with water and bring to the boil, then stir in the yeast extract until it dissolves. Continue cooking for a short time so that the 'mince meat' is soft, then drain and mix together with the mushrooms and noodles. Season generously.

6. Melt the margarine in a pan, then stir in the flour and cook gently until it begins to colour. Add the milk gradually, stirring continually, and continue cooking until the sauce thickens. Flavour with nutmeg and let cool for a short time before mixing with the other ingredients.

7. Take the pastry dough from the fridge, roll out, and use to line a good-sized flan dish. Prick with a fork and bake at 400°F/200°C (Gas Mark 6) for 10 minutes.

8. Remove from the oven and pour in the prepared filling, smoothing the top.

9. Make a decorative pattern with the sliced tomatoes, sprinkle with cheese, and return to the oven for 10-15 minutes more, or until the pastry is cooked. Serve hot.

BROCCOLI FLAN

Crostata di broccoli

Pastry:

Imperial (Metric)	American
6 oz (175g) plain wholemeal flour	1½ cupsful plain wholewheat flour
Pinch of nutmeg	Pinch of nutmeg
3 oz (75g) margarine or butter	⅓ cupful margarine or butter
1 egg	1 egg
Approx. 1 tablespoonful cold water	Approx. 1 tablespoonful cold water

Filling:

Imperial (Metric)	American
1 lb (450g) fresh or frozen broccoli	1 pound fresh or frozen broccoli
4 oz (100g) mushrooms	2 cupsful mushrooms
1 small onion	1 small onion
Seasoning to taste	Seasoning to taste
Pinch of nutmeg	Pinch of nutmeg
2 large eggs	2 large eggs
¼ pint (150ml) plain yogurt	⅔ cupful plain yogurt

1. Sift together the flour and nutmeg, and then use your fingertips to rub in the margarine until you have a mixture like fine crumbs.
2. Stir the beaten egg into the flour, then add just enough cold water to bind the ingredients to a dough. Knead it for a few minutes, wrap in aluminium foil or clingfilm, and set aside in the cool whilst you prepare the filling.
3. Wash and trim the broccoli. Break it into florets and steam for 5 minutes or until just cooked. Drain well, then chop coarsely.
4. Wash and slice the mushrooms.
5. Peel and chop the onion as fine as possible.

6. Combine the broccoli, mushrooms and onions, season to taste and add nutmeg.
7. Beat the eggs, stir in the yogurt gently.
8. Roll out the pastry and use it to line an 8 in. (20cm) flan dish. Pile the vegetables into the case, smooth the top, then pour on the egg and yogurt mixture, making sure it is evenly distributed.
9. Bake at 400°F/200°C (Gas Mark 6) for about 30 minutes, or until the filling is set and the pastry cooked. Serve hot.

4.
PEASANT FOODS

These are cheap, nutritious, filling foods that have served as staples for the poorer people of Italy for centuries. *Polenta* is very much a dish of the north, where the maize from which it is made grows easily and plentifully. *Gnocchi* are well known throughout the country, each area basing its version on whatever grows best within the province. Although few people are now so poor that they actually exist on these foods, both *polenta* and *gnocchi* are frequently served not just in private home, but in elegant restaurants too. The recipes may be adapted and expanded, the cookery techniques may be fancier, and most certainly diners will be served smaller portions, probably as a starter rather than as the main dish, but their popularity is in no way declining! Give them a try for yourself, you could well find them much tastier than you expect.

One point to remember about *polenta*: it is a yellow maize flour, and comes in various qualities from fine to coarse. Each quality requires a different amount of water in which to cook, the coarser requiring the most, so watch carefully when you cook *polenta*, and adjust the liquid accordingly. You can buy it at most health food and wholefood shops as well as Italian groceries and other specialist shops.

Buckwheat grows particularly well in one area of central Italy, and is much used there for various dishes, including *smacafam* (Buckwheat Pie), the recipe for which is given in this chapter, and *pasta di grano saraceno* (Buckwheat Pasta), the recipe for which is on page 95. A very simple yet unusual chick pea (garbanzo bean) dish is also given here, though there are a number of other recipes that include them scattered throughout the book.

CHEESE DUMPLINGS

Gnocchi di formaggio

Imperial (Metric)	American
½ lb (225g) Ricotta, cream or curd cheese	1 cupful Ricotta, cream or curd cheese
2 oz (50g) margarine or butter	5 tablespoonsful margarine or butter
2 eggs	2 eggs
2 oz (50g) grated Parmesan cheese	½ cupful grated Parmesan cheese
1 oz (25g) plain wholemeal flour	¼ cupful plain wholewheat flour
Pinch of nutmeg	Pinch of nutmeg
Seasoning to taste	Seasoning to taste
Plain wholemeal flour to coat	Plain wholewheat flour to coat

1. Beat the cheese until smooth and lump-free. Soften the margarine. Lightly beat the eggs.
2. Then mix together as thoroughly as possible the cheese, margarine, eggs, grated Parmesan, flour, nutmeg and seasoning. Cover the mixture and leave for at least a few hours in the fridge.
3. When ready to cook the *gnocchi*, use your hands to divide the mixture into small even-sized balls and roll them lightly in the flour.
4. Drop them a few at a time into a large pan of simmering salted water and cook for about 8 minutes, or until they rise to the surface. Remove with a slotted spoon and keep them warm whilst you cook the rest.

Note: Gnocchi can be served just as they are with a knob of butter, or with a tomato sauce, or a sprinkling of Parmesan cheese.

SPINACH DUMPLINGS

Gnocchi verdi

Imperial (Metric)

1 lb (450g) fresh spinach, or frozen equivalent
1 oz (25g) margarine or butter
Pinch of nutmeg
Seasoning to taste
6 oz (175g) Ricotta, cream or curd cheese
2 eggs
3 oz (75g) grated Parmesan cheese
1 oz (25g) plain wholemeal flour

American

1 pound fresh spinach, or frozen equivalent
2½ tablespoonsful margarine or butter
Pinch of nutmeg
Seasoning to taste
¾ cupful Ricotta, cream or curd cheese
2 eggs
¾ cupful grated Parmesan cheese
¼ cupful plain wholewheat flour

1. Cook the spinach in a small amount of water until tender, then drain well, chop finely and squeeze until it is as dry as you can make it.
2. Melt the margarine, add the spinach, nutmeg and seasoning, and cook over a low heat for a few minutes.
3. Mash the cheese and stir it into the spinach; continue cooking and stirring for a few minutes more.
4. Tip the mixture into a bowl, and cool slightly before beating in the eggs, ⅓ of the Parmesan cheese and most of the flour. When smooth and well blended set aside to chill for at least a few hours.
5. With floured hands, shape pieces of the soft mixture into small balls. Cook them a few at a time, in a large pan of simmering salted water. They should float to the top in 5-8 minutes, when they can be scooped out with a slotted spoon.
6. Keep the cooked *gnocchi verdi* warm while you use up the rest of the mixture. Serve hot sprinkled with the remaining Parmesan cheese.

POTATO DUMPLINGS

Gnocchi di patate

Imperial (Metric)
1 lb (450g) potatoes
6 oz (175g) plain wholemeal flour
1 egg
½ oz (12g) margarine or butter
Pinch of nutmeg
Seasoning to taste

American
1 pound potatoes
1½ cupsful plain wholewheat flour
1 egg
1 tablespoonful margarine or butter
Pinch of nutmeg
Seasoning to taste

1. Peel, slice and steam or boil the potatoes until soft enough to be mashed to a dry paste. Put this into a bowl and stir in most of the flour, lightly beaten egg, margarine, nutmeg and seasoning. You will end up with a fairly firm dough.
2. With floured hands, shape small pieces of the dough into pencil-like rolls, then break off into 1 in. (25mm) lengths and twist them into crescents.
3. Bring a large pan of salted water to the boil, drop the *gnocchi* into it, a few at a time, and cook about 5 minutes, or until they rise to the top. Remove them with a slotted spoon and place in a warm spot whilst you continue cooking the rest of the dough.
4. The simplest way to serve these *gnocchi di patate* is to top them with a knob or two of butter, a sprinkling of Parmesan cheese, and a pinch of cinnamon. If liked you can pop them very quickly under the grill, or in a medium oven. A more unusual way is to dilute a little pesto sauce (see page 101) with a few tablespoonsful of the water in which the *gnocchi* cooked, heat it gently, then pour it over them and serve at once.

SEMOLINA DUMPLINGS

Gnocchi di semolino

Imperial (Metric)	American
1 pint (550ml) milk	2½ cupsful milk
Pinch of nutmeg	Pinch of nutmeg
Seasoning to taste	Seasoning to taste
6 oz (175g) wholemeal semolina	1½ cupsful wholewheat semolina
4 oz (100g) grated Parmesan cheese	1 cupful grated Parmesan cheese
2 eggs	2 eggs
1 oz (25g) margarine or butter	2½ tablespoonsful margarine or butter

1. Put the milk into a saucepan with the nutmeg and seasoning, and bring to the boil.
2. Sprinkle in the semolina and continue cooking, stirring continuously, until the mixture becomes very thick.
3. Remove from the heat and cool slightly before adding half the cheese and the beaten eggs.
4. Lightly grease a flat tin (a Swiss-roll tin is ideal), pour in the mixture, and smooth the top. Leave to get completely cold — it can be left overnight if you like.
5. Use a cutter or small glass to cut the mixture into rounds and arrange them, overlapping slightly, in a greased ovenproof dish.
6. Top with knobs of margarine and the rest of the cheese, and bake at 400°F/200°C (Gas Mark 6) for 10-15 minutes. (Alternatively, you can put the gnocchi under the grill for a short time.) Serve at once.

SEMOLINA CHEESE FRITTERS

Gnocchi alla piemontese

1. Follow the recipe for *gnocchi di semolino*, adding 2 ounces (50g) grated Emmenthal cheese to the basic mixture with the Parmesan cheese. When cold, cut the dough into circles as described.
2. Dip them into a beaten egg, then into breadcrumbs so that they are well coated.
3. Deep fry in hot oil until crisp and brown, then drain on a paper towel and serve with either a tomato or béchamel sauce.

BREAD DUMPLINGS

Canederli

Imperial (Metric)	American
¾ lb (350g) wholemeal bread	¾ pound wholewheat bread
¼ pint (150ml) milk	⅔ cupful milk
2 small eggs	2 small eggs
2 oz (50g) plain wholemeal flour	½ cupful plain wholewheat flour
Fresh parsley	Fresh parsley
Seasoning to taste	Seasoning to taste
Vegetable stock	Vegetable stock
Grated Parmesan cheese to serve	Grated Parmesan cheese to serve

1. Crumble the bread and soak it for a short time in the milk, then squeeze it as dry as possible. Put the bread into a bowl and mix with the beaten eggs, flour, a generous amount of parsley and seasoning. Shape the mixture into small balls.
2. Heat the vegetable stock and drop in the *canederli* a few at a time, then cook for 5-8 minutes or until they float to the surface. Remove them with a slotted spoon and keep them warm whilst you cook the rest of the balls in the same way.
3. Serve hot sprinkled with cheese.

Note: Canederli are often flavoured with tiny bits of bacon when made in Italy, an idea you can follow by using soya 'bacon' bits. You can also make them into more of a meal by serving them topped with a tomato sauce, then adding a sprinkling of cheese, and putting them under the grill for a few minutes.

CHICK PEA BAKE
Farinata

Imperial (Metric)
½ lb (225g) chick pea or gram flour
1¼ pints (650ml) water
1 tablespoonful olive oil
Seasoning to taste

American
2 cupsful garbanzo bean or gram flour
3¼ cupsful water
1 tablespoonful olive oil
Seasoning to taste

1. Put the water into a saucepan with the flour, stir well, and cook gently for about 45 minutes, stirring frequently, until the mixture thickens. Season generously.
2. Oil a shallow tin (Swiss-roll size is ideal) and spoon in the mixture, smoothing the top before trickling it with the remainder of the oil.
3. Bake at 400°F/200°C (Gas Mark 6) for 20 minutes, or until firm and brown. Serve at once cut into squares.

Note: A tomato, parsley or cheese sauce goes deliciously well with this rather bland dish, which can also be made more interesting with the addition of your favourite herbs or spices.

CORNMEAL AND MUSHROOM BAKE

Polenta pasticciata

The wealthier Milanese sometimes use white truffles instead of mushrooms — but it's a tasty dish made either way.

Imperial (Metric)

1½ pints (¾ litre) water
Pinch of salt
½ lb (225g) fine polenta
Approx. 2 oz (50g) margarine or butter
1 oz (25g) plain wholemeal flour
1 pint (550ml) milk
Seasoning to taste
Pinch of nutmeg
½ lb (225g) mushrooms
2 oz (50g) grated Gruyère or other hard cheese

American

3¾ cupsful water
Pinch of salt
2 cupsful fine polenta
Approx. ¼ cupful margarine or butter
¼ cupful plain wholewheat flour
2½ cupsful milk
Seasoning to taste
Pinch of nutmeg
4 cupsful mushrooms
½ cupful grated Gruyère or other hard cheese

1. Bring the water to a boil, salt, then stir in the polenta using a wooden spoon. Cook for about 20 minutes, stirring frequently, until the mixture is thick. Pour into a shallow, lightly greased tin and set aside to cool.
2. Melt 1½ oz (35g) of the margarine and sprinklc with the flour. Cook briefly, then stir in the milk and continue cooking to make a creamy white sauce. Flavour with salt, pepper and nutmeg.
3. Use the rest of the margarine to gently fry the cleaned, sliced mushrooms for a few minutes so that they are tender but not overcooked.
4. Cut the polenta into small circles and layer half of it in a greased ovenproof dish.

5. Top with half of the mushrooms, then half of the sauce. Repeat this process to use up the rest of the ingredients, and sprinkle with the grated Gruyère cheese.

6. Bake at 350°F/180°C (Gas Mark 4) for about 30 minutes, or until bubbly. Serve immediately.

CORNMEAL SAVOURY

Polenta

Imperial (Metric)	American
1½ pints (¾ litre) water	3¾ cupsful water
Pinch of salt	Pinch of salt
½ lb (225g) fine polenta	2 cupsful fine polenta

1. Bring the water to the boil, add the salt, then use a wooden spoon to gradually stir in the polenta.

2. Continue cooking, stirring frequently, for 20-30 minutes. When the mixture is thick and smooth it is ready to eat. (It can also be cooked in a double boiler.)

Note: Polenta can be served in a wide variety of ways. Pour it into a shallow dish, dot with butter and sprinkle with cheese, and put under the grill for a minute or two. Serve it with a spicy pepper and tomato sauce, or cheese sauce. Or let it get cold, then cut it into rounds that can be fried until crisp and golden, baked in the oven, or grilled. You can also make a kind of *gnocchi* out of polenta.

BUCKWHEAT PIE

Smacafam

Imperial (Metric)	American
½ lb (225g) buckwheat	1 cupful buckwheat
1 pint (550ml) milk	2½ cupsful milk
4 onions	4 onions
3 tablespoonsful vegetable oil	3 tablespoonsful vegetable oil
Seasoning to taste	Seasoning to taste
1 oz (25g) grated Parmesan cheese	¼ cupful grated Parmesan cheese

1. In a heavy based saucepan toast the buckwheat over a medium heat for a few minutes, stirring with a wooden spoon, until the grains begin to colour.
2. Add the milk, bring to the boil, then cover and simmer for about 15 minutes until the buckwheat is tender. Season to taste.
3. Meanwhile, peel and slice the onions. Heat the oil in a separate pan and *sauté* the onions gently so that they soften but do not go brown.
4. Drain the buckwheat if there is any liquid left (most of it will probably have been absorbed), and transfer half of it to a greased ovenproof dish. Cover with half the onion. Add another layer of buckwheat, a second layer of onion.
5. Bake at 350°F/180°C (Gas Mark 4) for 10 minutes or until heated through. Sprinkle with cheese and serve hot.

Note: Smacafam is a nutritious but rather bland dish. The Italians often liven it up with spicy sausage meat, but you can achieve the same effect by adding any lightly cooked vegetable — green pepper and spinach both go especially well — and maybe some cooked beans or chopped nuts.

5.
RICE AND RISOTTOS

The north of Italy has an ideal climate for growing rice — which explains why Italy grows more of it than any other European country. And it is the northerners who consume it in the largest amounts, rice being to them what pasta is to the southerners.

The Italian risotto is a world-famous dish, though unfortunately it is usually made from white rice, a hangover from the days when 'refined' was another word for 'superior'. The situation is, however, gradually changing as the undoubted advantages of eating the whole grain are becoming known, and the Italians are keeping for themselves at least some of the huge quantity of brown rice they produce for the export market. As this trend increases, the character of the risotto will change or, it may be more accurate to say, go back to what it used to be. Meanwhile, if you eat a risotto in an Italian restaurant you can expect it to be rather more mushy than if it were made from brown rice, with its drier, firmer grains.

Use whichever you prefer in the dishes given here. Although white rice might taste more authentic, brown rice will be more tasty.

RICE WITH AUBERGINE

Riso con melanzane

Imperial (Metric)	American
1½ pints (¾ litre) vegetable stock	3¾ cupsful vegetable stock
10 oz (275g) brown rice	1¼ cupsful brown rice
1 large aubergine	1 large eggplant
3 tablespoonsful vegetable oil	3 tablespoonsful vegetable oil
1-2 clove garlic, crushed	1-2 cloves garlic, crushed
4 oz (100g) mushrooms	2 cupsful mushrooms
Parsley	Parsley
Seasoning to taste	Seasoning to taste
Green olives (optional)	Green olives (optional)
Grated cheese to serve	Grated cheese to serve

1. Bring vegetable stock to the boil and add the rice. Lower heat and cover pan, then leave to cook for about 20 minutes, or until rice is ready.
2. Meanwhile, peel and dice the aubergine (eggplant). Heat the oil and *sauté* the crushed garlic for a few minutes before adding the aubergine (eggplant). Cook gently for 10 minutes, stirring frequently.
3. Add the cleaned, chopped mushrooms and a handful of chopped parsley, mix well, and cook 5 minutes more. (If the mixture seems rather dry, pour in an extra spoonful of oil.) Season to taste.
4. When both the rice and aubergine (eggplant) mixture are cooked, drain the rice and put it into a warmed serving bowl. Pour the vegetables over the top and sprinkle with a few green olives, if liked. Hand the grated cheese around the table so everyone can help themselves.

Note: Although it is traditional to serve cheese with this dish, it is also delicious with either chopped hard-boiled eggs, green peas or chick peas (garbanzo beans).

VENETIAN RICE AND PEAS

Risi e bisi

Sometimes this is made into a soup by the addition of more stock. The version given here is intended to be eaten with a fork, but you can easily adapt it if you want to try it both ways.

Imperial (Metric)
1 oz (25g) margarine or butter
2 tablespoonsful vegetable oil
1 small onion
Parsley
1 lb (450g) shelled fresh peas, or frozen equivalent
10 oz (275g) brown rice
1½ pints (¾ litre) vegetable stock
Grated cheese or soya 'bacon bits' to serve

American
2½ tablespoonsful margarine or butter
2 tablespoonsful vegetable oil
1 small onion
Parsley
2⅔ cupsful shelled fresh peas, or frozen equivalent
1¼ cupsful brown rice
3¾ cupsful vegetable stock
Grated cheese or soy 'bacon bits' to serve

1. In a large pan, gently heat the margarine and oil. Cook the chopped onion briefly, add the parsley and continue cooking until the onion becomes transparent.
2. Add the peas and rice, stirring so that they are coated with the fat, then pour in the vegetable stock and bring it to the boil.
3. Reduce the heat and simmer the rice mixture for about 20 minutes, or until all the ingredients are cooked, and most (if not all) of the liquid has been absorbed.
4. Serve with grated Parmesan cheese, or sprinkled with soya 'bacon bits' — the Venetians may well eat it with both cheese and *prosciutto* (ham).

DEEP-FRIED RICE BALLS

Suppli di riso

Imperial (Metric)
6 oz (175g) brown rice
1 pint (550ml) vegetable stock or water
2 tomatoes
Seasoning to taste
2 eggs
4 oz (100g) Mozzarella cheese
3-4 oz (75-100g) fine wholemeal breadcrumbs
Oil for frying

American
3/4 cupful brown rice
2½ cupsful vegetable stock or water
2 tomatoes
Seasoning to taste
2 eggs
4 ounces Mozzarella cheese
1½-2 cupsful fine wholewheat breadcrumbs
Oil for frying

1. Add the rice to the boiling stock or water, stir in the peeled and finely chopped tomatoes and then simmer the mixture until the rice is cooked. Add seasoning. Drain well and leave to cool.
2. Beat the eggs and add them to the rice mixture. Put a tablespoonful of it onto the palm of your hand, put a cube or piece of cheese on top, then mould the rice around the cheese to form a small ball. Roll this very carefully in the breadcrumbs to make a light, even coating. Use up the rest of the ingredients in the same way.
3. Deep fry the balls a few at a time in a deep pan of hot oil, turning them frequently, until the outsides are golden and crisp — the cheese inside will melt to a thick cream. Drain the rice balls on paper towels and serve whilst still hot.

Note: Make these when you have plain rice or risotto left over from a previous meal, and cut the preparation time in half. Just make sure there are no large pieces of vegetables in the rice which may tend to make the mixture more crumbly.

RED AND GREEN RISOTTO

Risotto con peperoni

Imperial (Metric)

4 tablespoonsful vegetable oil
1 small onion
2 small red peppers
2 small green peppers
2 sticks of celery
2 tomatoes
Basil
Seasoning to taste
10 oz (275g) brown rice
1½ pints (¾ litre) vegetable stock
1 oz (25g) margarine or butter
1 oz (25g) pistachio nuts

American

⅓ cupful vegetable oil
1 small onion
2 small red peppers
2 small green peppers
2 sticks of celery
2 tomatoes
Basil
Seasoning to taste
1¼ cupsful brown rice
3¾ cupsful vegetable stock
2½ tablespoonsful margarine or butter
¼ cupful pistachio nuts

1. Heat the oil in a saucepan, slice the onion, dice the peppers, chop the celery stalks, and add them all to the oil. Stir well, then cover and cook on a medium heat for 15 minutes, checking that the mixture does not get too dry (if it does, add a tiny drop of water).

2. Stir in the coarsely chopped tomatoes, basil and seasoning and the rice; cook a minute more. Add the vegetable stock, bring to the boil then cover and simmer for 30 minutes, or until the rice is cooked.

3. Transfer the risotto to a serving dish, top with knobs of butter and a sprinkling of the nuts. Pistachios look especially good with this dish, but if you cannot find (or afford) them, use whatever nuts you have handy.

RICE WITH TRUFFLES

Riso con tartufi bianchi

Truffles are a kind of mushroom that grow underground in just a few parts of Italy. Because they are so rare, they are very expensive, and are therefore treated with great respect when used in a dish. This simple recipe is a popular way of serving the delicately flavoured white truffle.

Imperial (Metric)	**American**
10 oz (275g) brown rice*	1¼ cupsful brown rice*
1½ pints (¾ litre) vegetable stock	3¾ cupsful vegetable stock
4-6 oz (100-175g) freshly grated Parmesan cheese	1-1½ cupsful freshly grated Parmesan cheese
2 oz (50g) unsalted butter	5 tablespoonsful unsalted butter
Seasoning to taste	Seasoning to taste
White truffles**	White truffles**

1. Simmer the rice in the vegetable stock until it is perfectly cooked — tender but not mushy.
2. Drain, and stir in the cheese, butter and seasoning.
3. When the cheese and butter have melted to make the rice creamy smooth, transfer it to a warmed serving dish, and top with paper thin slices of the raw truffles. Serve at once.

*Although brown rice is more nutritious, it has a stronger flavour than the white variety, which may diminish the subtle garlic-like taste of the truffles.

**Use as many truffles as you can find and afford. Even one truffle added to rice in this way makes it a very special dish.

BAKED RICE DISH

Risotto arrosto

Imperial (Metric)	American
4 oz (100g) margarine or butter	½ cupful margarine or butter
1 small onion	1 small onion
6 oz (175g) shelled fresh peas, or frozen equivalent	1 cupful shelled fresh peas, or frozen equivalent
2 cooked artichoke hearts	2 cooked artichoke hearts
3 oz (75g) mushrooms	1½ cupsful mushrooms
½ pint (275ml) water	1¼ cupsful water
¾ lb (350g) brown rice	1½ cupsful brown rice
2 oz (50g) grated Parmesan cheese	½ cupful grated Parmesan cheese
Oregano to taste	Oregano to taste
Seasoning to taste	Seasoning to taste

1. Melt half the margarine in a saucepan and fry the sliced onion gently for 5 minutes.
2. Add the peas, coarsely chopped artichoke hearts, sliced mushrooms and water, and simmer for 15 minutes.
3. In a separate pan, cook the rice in water for about 15 minutes.
4. Drain well then stir into the vegetables — the mixture should be moist but not too wet. Flavour with oregano and season to taste, then transfer to an ovenproof dish. Dot the top with the rest of the margarine and sprinkle with the cheese.
5. Bake at 400°F/200°C (Gas Mark 6) for 15-20 minutes, or until the rice is tender and the top lightly browned. (You can put it under the grill for a few minutes to give it a crustier topping, if liked.) Serve hot.

COURGETTES WITH RICE FILLING

Zucchini ripieni di riso

Imperial (Metric)

3 tablespoonsful vegetable oil
1 onion
6 oz (175g) brown rice
1 pint (550ml) vegetable stock or water
4 medium courgettes
Parsley
Seasoning to taste
2 oz (50g) pine nuts or chopped roasted hazelnuts
2 tablespoonsful dry white wine (optional)

American

3 tablespoonsful vegetable oil
1 onion
¾ cupful brown rice
2½ cupsful vegetable stock or water
4 medium zucchini
Parsley
Seasoning to taste
4 tablespoonsful pine nuts or chopped roasted hazelnuts
2 tablespoonsful dry white wine (optional)

1. Heat half the oil in a saucepan, add the chopped onion and *sauté* briefly, then stir in the rice. Cook for a few minutes before adding the vegetable stock, bring to the boil, then simmer for 20 minutes, or until rice is tender.

2. Meanwhile, parboil the courgettes (zucchini) in boiling water for 5 minutes, drain and dry. Cut them in half lengthways and scoop out a little of the flesh to leave a long hollow in each. (This can be reserved for use in another dish, such as vegetable soup, or chop it finely and add to the rice whilst it cooks.) Arrange the shells in an ovenproof dish.

3. When the rice is ready, drain it well, then mix with the parsley, season to taste, and stir in the nuts. Pile some of the mixture into each of the prepared shells, and sprinkle each one with a drop of the remaining oil, and some white wine.

4. Bake at 375°F/190°C (Gas Mark 5) for 30-40 minutes, or until the courgettes (zucchini) are completely cooked. They can be eaten hot or cold. For extra protein, add some grated cheese to the rice mixture, or sprinkle it over the cooked courgettes (zucchini) and brown under a hot grill.

SUMMER RICE DISH

Risotto 'Estate'

Imperial (Metric)	American
2 tablespoonsful vegetable oil	2 tablespoonsful vegetable oil
1 onion	1 onion
1 medium courgette	1 medium zucchini
4 oz (100g) broad beans	2/3 cupful Windsor beans
4 oz (100g) green beans	4 ounces green beans
1/2 small cabbage	1/2 small cabbage
1/2 lb (225g) brown rice	1 cupful brown rice
1 1/4 pints (650ml) vegetable stock	3 1/4 cupsful vegetable stock
2 tomatoes	2 tomatoes
Seasoning to taste	Seasoning to taste
1 oz (25g) margarine or butter	2 1/2 tablespoonsful margarine or butter
Chives to garnish	Chives to garnish
Grated cheese (optional)	Grated cheese (optional)

1. Heat the oil in a large pan and gently fry the sliced onion for a few minutes.
2. Add the sliced courgette (zucchini), the broad (Windsor) beans, chopped green beans, and shredded cabbage, and mix well.
3. Cover the pan and cook gently for 5 minutes more.
4. Stir in the rice and cook briefly until it becomes translucent.
5. Pour in the stock, and continue cooking until the rice is tender and the liquid has been absorbed.
6. Add the quartered tomatoes and leave the pan over a gentle heat for just a minute more so that they are heated through but not cooked.
7. Off the heat, stir in the margarine so that it melts to give the rice a creamy coating. Tip it into a warmed dish, top with chopped chives, and serve immediately. Grated cheese could be handed round at the table.

LEMON RICE WITH EGG

Riso al limone e uova

Imperial (Metric)
½ lb (225g) brown rice
2 eggs
2 tablespoonsful lemon juice
2 oz (50g) grated Parmesan cheese
Seasoning to taste
1 oz (25g) margarine or butter

American
1 cupful brown rice
2 eggs
2 tablespoonsful lemon juice
½ cupful grated Parmesan cheese
Seasoning to taste
2½ tablespoonsful margarine or butter

1. Cook the rice in a good quantity of water (or vegetable stock) until just tender.
2. Meanwhile, beat the eggs together in a bowl until light and frothy, then beat in the lemon juice, cheese and seasoning.
3. Drain the cooked rice well. Melt the margarine in a saucepan and add the rice, stirring it so that the grains are coated evenly.
4. Over a very low heat, gradually add the egg and lemon mixture to the rice, and continue to cook it, stirring occasionally, for a few minutes. When the eggs have cooked sufficiently to make a creamy sauce, serve at once.

Note: This is a rich-tasting recipe, so the quantities suggested are slightly smaller than usual. Serve it with a crisp (and maybe nutty) salad for a balanced meal. It is also a good dish for anyone who has trouble digesting their food, or for convalescents.

RICE SALAD

Insalata di riso

Imperial (Metric)

½ lb (225g) brown rice
1 pint (550ml) water or vegetable stock
1 yellow pepper
2 large tomatoes
½ cucumber
2 sticks celery
2 carrots
2 spring onions
1 tablespoonful capers
10 black olives
4 tablespoonsful olive oil
1 tablespoonful wine vinegar
Seasoning to taste
Chicory or curly endive lettice

American

1 cupful brown rice
2½ cupsful water or vegetable stock
1 yellow pepper
2 large tomatoes
½ cucumber
2 sticks celery
2 carrots
2 scallions
1 tablespoonful capers
10 black olives
⅓ cupful olive oil
1 tablespoonful wine vinegar
Seasoning to taste
Chicory or curly endive lettuce

1. Add the rice to the boiling water or stock and cook for about 20 minutes, or until tender. Drain well and set aside.
2. Slice the pepper, quarter the tomatoes, cube the cucumber and chop the celery and carrot into small slices. Cut the onions as fine as possible. Mix all the prepared vegetables plus the capers and olives into the rice.
3. Whisk the oil and vinegar together, add seasoning and stir them into the rice salad, mixing very thoroughly.
4. When ready to serve, arrange the chicory leaves or lettuce around the edges of a shallow dish, and pile the rice in the middle. If liked, reserve the tomatoes and olives and use them to decorate the salad rather than mixing them in with the other ingredients.

6.
VEGETABLE DISHES

The Italian climate and soil are ideal for growing a wide variety of sweet and flavoursome vegetables, which therefore feature frequently in Italian cookery. And because they are such good quality vegetables, they are rarely relegated to a supporting role. Usually they are served as a separate dish to be enjoyed in its own right, either at the start of the meal, or midway through it.

Unfortunately, many Italians still follow the tradition of boiling or steaming their vegetables, then frying them in butter before serving — a practice that takes away much of the natural taste as well as the goodness. Few of the recipes given here follow this method.

You will notice that certain items crop up again and again, and it must be admitted that the Italians are especially fond of some vegetables — tomatoes, aubergines (eggplants), onions, peppers, courgettes (zucchini) — so much so that you would think they would grow tired of them. They don't because the vegetables are served in so many different guises, it's sometimes hard to recognize them.

One vegetable that is not widely used in Italy is the potato. When it does appear on the table it is usually as a creamy *purée*, or in potato croquettes — though for the tourist trade, the Italians have learned how to make chips!

FRIED COURGETTES WITH ALMONDS

Zucchini fritti con mandorle

Imperial (Metric)
1 lb (450g) courgettes
1 oz (25g) margarine or butter
1 tablespoonful vegetable oil
4 tablespoonsful dry white wine or vegetable stock
Squeeze of lemon juice
2 oz (50g) blanched almonds
Seasoning to taste
1 oz (25g) sesame seeds

American
1 pound zucchini
2½ tablespoonsful margarine or butter
1 tablespoonful vegetable oil
⅓ cupful dry white wine or vegetable stock
Squeeze of lemon juice
½ cupful blanched almonds
Seasoning to taste
2 tablespoonsful sesame seeds

1. Wash, dry and cut the courgettes (zucchini) into fairly thick slices.
2. Heat together the margarine and oil and, when hot, add the courgettes (zucchini) and *sauté* for a few minutes, turning frequently so that they colour evenly.
3. Pour in the wine and lemon juice and cook a few minutes more, or until the courgettes (zucchini) begin to soften.
4. Add the nuts and seasoning, and heat through. Serve at once, sprinkled lightly with sesame seeds.

BAKED FENNEL

Finocchi al forno con formaggio

Imperial (Metric)	American
4 medium fennel bulbs	4 medium fennel bulbs
1/3 pint (200ml) vegetable stock	3/4 cupful vegetable stock
2 oz (50g) margarine or butter	5 tablespoonsful margarine or butter
Seasoning to taste	Seasoning to taste
2 oz (50g) grated Gruyère, or other hard cheese	1/2 cupful grated Gruyère, or other hard cheese
1 oz (25g) wholemeal breadcrumbs	1/2 cupful wholewheat breadcrumbs

1. Trim the base of the fennel bulbs, and cut away any tough leaves. Cut them lengthways into halves, then cut each half into two or three chunks. Lay these in the base of a shallow, lightly greased ovenproof dish.
2. Pour on the vegetable stock, dot most of the margarine over the fennel, and season generously. Sprinkle with the grated cheese.
3. Cover the dish and bake the fennel at 350°F/180°C (Gas Mark 4) for 40-50 minutes, or until tender.
4. Scatter the breadcrumbs over the top, dot with the rest of the fat, and either return the dish to the oven for 10 minutes, or place under a hot grill.

SWEET-SOUR VEGETABLES
Caponata

Imperial (Metric)
2 large aubergines
6 tablespoonsful olive oil
1 large onion
4 large sticks celery, parboiled
1 lb (450g) tomatoes
10-15 green olives, halved and stoned
1 oz (25g) raw cane sugar
3 tablespoonsful wine vinegar
2 tablespoonsful capers
Seasoning to taste
4 hard-boiled eggs or 2 oz (50g) almonds or pine nuts (optional)

American
2 large eggplants
½ cupful olive oil
1 large onion
4 large sticks celery, parboiled
1 pound tomatoes
10-15 green olives, halved and stoned
2 tablespoonsful raw cane sugar
3 tablespoonsful wine vinegar
2 tablespoonsful capers
Seasoning to taste
4 hard-boiled eggs or 4 tablespoonsful almonds or pine nuts (optional)

1. Dice the aubergines (eggplants), sprinkle lightly with salt, and set aside for an hour. Then rinse with cold water and pat dry.
2. Heat half the oil in a large pan and fry the aubergine (eggplant) cubes until golden, turning them frequently. Drain on paper towels.
3. Chop the onion, celery and tomatoes. Add the remainder of the oil to the pan, and then *sauté* the onion for a few minutes before stirring in the celery, tomatoes and olives. Simmer until the celery is cooked.
4. Add the sugar, vinegar, capers, seasoning, and the aubergine (eggplant) cubes, and cook gently for 10 minutes more, or until the liquid thickens to become a light sauce. Adjust the seasoning if necessary.

Note: Caponata is usually served cold and unadorned, although sliced eggs or nuts are sometimes arranged on top of the vegetables, and so provide the protein needed if it is to be your main dish. It is also amazingly good eaten hot.

POTATO CROQUETTES

Crocchette di patate

This is one of the most widely used ways of serving potatoes in Italy.

Imperial (Metric)

1 lb (450g) potatoes
1 oz (25g) margarine or butter
1 oz (25g) grated Parmesan cheese
2 eggs, lightly beaten
Pinch of basil
Pinch of rosemary
Seasoning to taste
Approx. 2 oz (50g) crisp wholemeal breadcrumbs
Vegetable oil for frying

American

1 pound potatoes
2½ tablespoonsful margarine or butter
¼ cupful grated Parmesan cheese
2 eggs, lightly beaten
Pinch of basil
Pinch of rosemary
Seasoning to taste
Approx. 1 cupful crisp wholewheat breadcrumbs
Vegetable oil for frying

1. Peel, cube, and boil or steam the potatoes until soft.
2. Drain them well, then mash or sieve to make a thick paste. Whilst this is still warm stir in the margarine and cheese.
3. Cool slightly, then add half the lightly beaten egg, herbs and seasoning to taste. Set the mixture aside to get completely cold.
4. Shape the potato into croquettes, dip them into the remainder of the beaten egg, then roll in the crumbs so that they are well coated.
5. Heat the vegetable oil in a good-sized pan and gently deep fry your *crocchette*, a few at a time, until they are golden in colour, and firm in texture. Drain on paper towels and serve whilst still hot.

STUFFED ONIONS

Cipolle farcite

Imperial (Metric)
4 medium onions
2 tablespoonsful wholemeal breadcrumbs
1 oz (25g) pine nuts
1 oz (25g) sultanas
Parsley
Seasoning to taste
1-2 tablespoonsful vegetable oil
2 oz (50g) grated cheese (optional)

American
4 medium onions
2 tablespoonsful wholewheat breadcrumbs
¼ cupful pine nuts
3 tablespoonsful golden seedless raisins
Parsley
Seasoning to taste
1-2 tablespoonsful vegetable oil
½ cupful grated cheese (optional)

1. Peel onions carefully, then cook them in boiling water for 15 minutes. Drain well, cool slightly, then cut them crossways into even halves. Scoop out most of the onion flesh leaving a firm shell.
2. Chop some of the onion and add it to the breadcrumbs. Mix in the pine nuts, sultanas (golden seedless raisins), a good handful of fresh parsley, and seasoning. Use a drop of vegetable oil to moisten the mixture.
3. Stand the onion shells close together in a lightly greased ovenproof dish, and pile a generous amount of filling back into each one. Top them, if you like, with grated cheese.
4. Bake at 400°F/200°C (Gas Mark 6) for 20-30 minutes, and serve straight away.

Note: For a completely different version of *cipolle farcite*, fill the onion shells with a lentil mixture (such as described on page 115), and serve with a tomato sauce.

TUSCANY-STYLE BEANS

Fagioli alla Toscana

Imperial (Metric)	**American**
1½ lb (¾ kilo) fresh broad beans	1½ pounds fresh Windsor beans
4 tablespoonsful olive oil	⅓ cupful olive oil
2 cloves garlic, crushed	2 cloves garlic, crushed
2 sprigs sage	2 sprigs sage
Seasoning to taste	Seasoning to taste
10 oz (275g) fresh tomatoes or ½ lb (225g) tinned tomatoes	10 ounces fresh tomatoes or 1 cupful tinned tomatoes

1. Shell the beans and set them aside.
2. Heat the oil in a large frying pan (skillet), add the garlic and sage, and fry gently for a few minutes. Stir in the prepared beans and seasoning, and let stand for a few minutes more.
3. Meanwhile, skin and chop the tomatoes very finely (if using the tinned variety mash them, or push through a sieve). Add these to the beans, mixing well, then return the pan to the heat, cover, and simmer 15-20 minutes, stirring occasionally. Remove the sprigs of sage before serving. *Fagioli alla Toscana* is eaten hot or cold.

Note: Other beans are often used instead of broad (Windsor) beans, canellini or borlotti being especially popular. If you wish to use left-over or tinned beans, follow the same recipe but cook them for only 10 minutes. You can also substitute dried sage for the fresh sage sprigs — though an Italian would assure you that it will not taste nearly as good!

CAULIFLOWER WITH EGG SAUCE

Cavolfiore in salsa d'uovo

Imperial (Metric)
1 large cauliflower
1½ oz (35g) margarine or butter
1 clove garlic, crushed
2 eggs
½ oz (12g) plain wholemeal flour
Seasoning to taste
1 tablespoonful white wine vinegar

American
1 large cauliflower
3½ tablespoonsful margarine or butter
1 clove garlic, crushed
2 eggs
2 tablespoonsful plain wholewheat flour
Seasoning to taste
1 tablespoonful white wine vinegar

1. Break the cauliflower into large florets and steam or boil until they are just cooked.
2. At the same time prepare the sauce. Melt the margarine in a saucepan and add the crushed garlic, cooking it gently for 5 minutes.
3. In a bowl, beat the eggs and flour together. Season to taste and stir in the white wine vinegar.
4. Add to the saucepan, mix well, then remove it from the heat and beat energetically until the sauce is creamy and smooth.
5. Transfer the drained cauliflower to an attractive dish and pour the sauce over the top. Serve at once.

Note: Broccoli can be served in the same way, and makes a delicious change.

AUBERGINE CHEESE ROLLS

Rollini di melanzane alla besciamella

Rolls:

Imperial (Metric)	**American**
4 medium aubergines	4 medium eggplants
Salt	Salt
Approx. 2 oz (50g) wholemeal flour	Approx. ½ cupful wholewheat flour
Vegetable oil for frying	Vegetable oil for frying
½ lb (225g) Ricotta cheese	1 cupful Ricotta cheese

Sauce:

Imperial (Metric)	**American**
2 oz (50g) margarine or butter	5 tablespoonsful margarine or butter
2 oz (50g) plain wholemeal flour	½ cupful plain wholewheat flour
1 pint (550ml) milk	2½ cupsful milk
Seasoning to taste	Seasoning to taste
1 oz (25g) grated Parmesan cheese	¼ cupful grated Parmesan cheese
2 egg yolks	2 egg yolks

1. Wash the aubergines (eggplants), trim the bases, then cut lengthways into very thin slices. Lay them on a plate, sprinkle with salt, and leave for 30 minutes. Rinse thoroughly in cold water, then pat the slices with paper towels to dry.
2. Coat them evenly in flour and fry quickly in vegetable oil until lightly browned on each side. Drain well on paper towels and leave to cool.
3. Roll each of the slices up, placing a small amount of the cheese in the centre of each roll. Arrange them close together in an ovenproof dish — if you like you can secure the rolls with a skewer or toothpick, but it should not really be necessary.
4. To make the sauce, melt the margarine and *sauté* the flour in it for a few minutes. Stir in the milk, and continue stirring as it comes to the boil.

5. When the sauce is thick and completely smooth remove it from the heat and cool slightly before adding the seasoning, grated cheese and egg yolks. Mix well. Pour the sauce over the rolls making sure it is evenly distributed.

6. Bake at 375°F/190°C (Gas Mark 5) for about 10 minutes, or until heated through.

Note: This is a very rich dish so the amount given here could well be enough for 6 servings. If you cannot obtain Ricotta cheese, you could just omit it and still produce a tasty dish. A tomato sauce instead of the *besciamella* is also frequently served in Italian homes.

MIXED FRIED VEGETABLES

Fritto misto di verdure

For this popular way of serving vegetables in Italy, you can use just about any variety you fancy — and there are almost as many recipes for different batters! This one is especially light and crisp, others are more filling and many contain wine or even beer.

Choose three or four from such vegetables as:

Courgettes (zucchini)
Cauliflower
Aubergine (eggplant)
Celery sticks
Artichoke hearts (fresh or tinned)
Fennel
Carrots
Mushrooms

Batter:

Imperial (Metric)	**American**
4 oz (100g) plain wholemeal flour	1 cupful plain wholewheat flour
3 tablespoonsful vegetable oil	3 tablespoonsful vegetable oil
Pinch of salt	Pinch of salt
¼ pint (150ml) warm water	⅔ cupful warm water
1 egg white	1 egg white
Vegetable oil for frying	Vegetable oil for frying

1. Use a spoon to mix together the flour, oil, salt and water, then beat the batter to make sure it is smooth as well as to add air. Set aside in the cool, preferably for a few hours.

2. Prepare the vegetables. The courgettes (zucchini) should be washed, trimmed, and either cut into round slices, or cut lengthways into thick, even-sized strips. Break the cauliflower into florets. Peel and halve the aubergine (eggplant) lengthways, then cut into strips. Chop the cleaned celery into 2 in. (5cm) pieces. The artichoke hearts should be small enough, and will just need to be well drained. Trim the base and outer leaves of the fennel, then cut lengthways into small chunks. Cut the peeled carrots into thick strips. Button mushrooms can be left whole, larger ones should be halved or even quartered.

3. Although most of the vegetables do not need to be pre-cooked as they will cook briefly in the oil (and in any case should be quite crisp when eaten) you can — if you like — *blanch* the tougher varieties for 2 minutes in boiling water. Drain them well and cool before using.

4. When ready to cook your *fritto misto*, beat the batter lightly again, then add the stiffly beaten egg white. Dip the vegetables into the batter, then drop a few at a time into a large saucepan of very hot vegetable oil, lower the heat a little, and cook for about 5 minutes, turning occasionally.

5. When the batter has turned golden and is puffed up, remove the vegetables with a slotted spoon and drain well on paper towels. Although they can be kept warm whilst you cook the remaining *fritto misto*, they are best served as hot and freshly-made as possible.

GREEN PEPPER AND PARMESAN BAKE

Parmigianata di peperoni

Imperial (Metric)	American
Parsley	Parsley
1 lb (450g) tomatoes	1 pound tomatoes
3 tablespoonsful vegetable oil	3 tablespoonsful vegetable oil
4 green peppers	4 green peppers
1 clove garlic, crushed	1 clove garlic, crushed
1 large onion	1 large onion
Seasoning to taste	Seasoning to taste
6 oz (175g) Mozzarella cheese	6 ounces Mozzarella cheese
3 oz (75g) grated Parmesan cheese	¾ cupful grated Parmesan cheese

1. Chop the parsley; peel and either chop the tomatoes or press them through a sieve to make a sauce, and stir in the parsley.
2. Heat the oil in a large frying pan (skillet). Remove the seeds from the peppers, wash and dry them, then cut lengthways into wide strips, and add to the pan. Add the garlic and cook for a few minutes, stirring frequently, then stir in the chopped onion. Continue cooking over a low heat until the vegetables are tender but not browned. Season to taste.
3. Take an ovenproof dish and lay half of the pepper and onion across the base. Top it with half the Mozzarella cheese cut into slices, then pour on half of the tomato sauce. Repeat this to use up the rest of the ingredients, then sprinkle a thick layer of Parmesan cheese over the top.
4. Bake at 350°F/180°C (Gas Mark 4) for 20 minutes, or until heated through. Serve at once.

Note: This basic recipe can also be adapted to use other vegetables. *Parmigianata di melanzane* is made with sliced of fried aubergine (eggplant), *Parmigianata di finocchi* with fennel and *Parmigianata di zucchini* with courgettes (zucchini).

7.
PASTAS

The durum wheat that is used for most of Italy's pasta grows in Sicily, so it is natural that the southerners should be especially fond of it — have been, in fact, since Roman times. They eat pasta in the north too, though tend to make theirs without eggs. Most Italians will eat pasta at least once a day, choosing from white, green, or wholemeal, and some 50 different forms ranging from tiny stars to spirals to wide flat strips. Just to confuse matters, the names of many of the different varieties change from one province to the next!

Italians may buy their pasta ready-made and dried, in packets, but they usually prefer to buy it from the many stores throughout the country that have it freshly made for them every day. There are also still many housewives who enjoy making their own pasta — and whose families enjoy the difference this makes to their meals.

Here are a few points to consider if trying to decide whether to use white or wholemeal pasta. Most Italians still use white, so that kind will taste more authentic, but wholemeal pasta contains more protein as well as fibre, so it is better for you. Its coarser texture makes it more filling, so you need to use less of it. And because of using less, you'll consume fewer calories — though if you are watching your weight, look out for the sauces, they are usually much more fattening than the pasta!

The following recipes recommend certain kinds of pasta to be used for each, but in most cases you can substitute another variety without ruining the dish. What *can* ruin the dish is overcooking the pasta. The time it takes will vary considerably. If using dried pasta, follow the instructions on the packet. If it is home-made, cook it a shorter time than for the dried variety. Test after a few minutes — the best way is to bite a piece, and if it feels tender but still firm (a texture the Italians call *al dente*), remove it from the heat at once.

EGG PASTA

Pasta all'uovo

Imperial (Metric)	**American**
½ lb (225g) plain wholemeal flour	2 cupsful plain wholewheat flour
Pinch of salt	Pinch of salt
2 eggs	2 eggs
1 tablespoonful vegetable oil	1 tablespoonful vegetable oil
Cold water to mix	Cold water to mix

1. Sift the flour and salt into a bowl. Make a well in the centre, beat the eggs and oil together lightly, and mix into the flour.
2. Use your hands to knead the dough so that it becomes smooth and pliable, adding a few drops of water as you do so to encourage the ingredients to bind together. Cover the dough or wrap in greaseproof paper, and set aside for 30 minutes or longer.
3. When ready to roll out your pasta, divide it into two to make it easier to handle. Roll out carefully on a lightly floured board, dusting the surface with extra flour if it is sticky, until the dough is as thin as you can make it. Brush off excess flour, then shape as required. Set aside to dry for 10-15 minutes.

Note: Home-made pasta is best used the same day, but if necessary it can be kept in the refrigerator, wrapped in polythene, for up to 2 days.

GREEN PASTA

Pasta verde

Imperial (Metric)	**American**
Ingredients as for *pasta all'uovo*	Ingredients as for *pasta all'uovo*
4 oz (100g) spinach	4 ounces spinach

1. Sift the flour and salt, and set aside.
2. Wash the spinach and cook, without adding extra water, for 5 minutes or until soft. Drain the spinach, squeeze it to remove all the water, then push through a sieve or *purée* in a blender.
3. Beat it with the eggs and oil, add to the flour, and proceed as with basic egg pasta recipe.

BUCKWHEAT PASTA

Pasta di grano saraceno

Imperial (Metric)	**American**
6 oz (175g) buckwheat flour	1½ cupsful buckwheat flour
2 oz (50g) plain wholemeal flour	½ cupful plain wholewheat flour
Pinch of salt	Pinch of salt
1 large egg	1 large egg
3 tablespoonsful milk	3 tablespoonsful milk
Warm water to mix	Warm water to mix

1. Sift together the two flours and the salt.
2. Beat the egg with the milk, and add to the dry ingredients with just enough warm water to make a firm but pliable dough. Knead for a few minutes, then cover and set aside for at least 30 minutes.
3. Roll out the prepared dough as thin as possible before cutting it into the pasta variety of your choice. Although *pasta di grano saraceno* can be used in any pasta dish, Italians tend to use it mostly cut into long thin strips such as noodles or tagliatelle.

SHAPING YOUR PASTA

To make ribbon pastas:

Roll out the pasta dough as thin as possible, dust lightly with flour, then roll the dough into a long sausage shape. Use a very sharp knife to cut the roll into ribbon-like strips about ¼ in. (6mm) wide for *tagliatelle*, narrower still for *noodles*. Try not to press too hard or the layers may stick together. Carefully unroll the strips of dough and lay them out on a clean cloth until required.

To make flat pastas:

Roll out the pasta dough as thin as possible, then use a sharp knife to cut into the shapes you require. For *lasagne* cut it into oblongs about 3 × 7 in. (8 × 18cm), or to fit the dish you intend to use. For *cannelloni*, cut the pasta into strips about 3 × 4 in. (8 × 10cm); this is a convenient size for rolling into tubes around the filling of your choice. For *ravioli* simply roll the dough flat, mark into squares and dot with the filling, then cover with a second sheet of dough (see page 104).

To make shaped pastas:

Unusual shaped pastas are fun to make as well as to eat. *Farfaletti*, for example, are little bows made by cutting the dough into strips 3 × 1 in. (8 × 2.5cm), then pinching the centres. A serrated-edged pastry wheel makes them even prettier. Use a special cutter and you can make stars, rings, wheels, letters of the alphabet — whatever you fancy.

To make tubular pastas:

Pastas such as spaghetti and macaroni can only be made at home if you have a pasta making machine.

SICILIAN-STYLE PASTA

Vermicelli alla Siciliana

Imperial (Metric)	**American**
1 green pepper	1 green pepper
6 tablespoonsful olive oil	½ cupful olive oil
2 cloves garlic	2 cloves garlic
½ medium aubergine	½ medium eggplant
¾ lb (350g) fresh tomatoes	¾ pound fresh tomatoes
1 tablespoonful capers	1 tablespoonful capers
12 black olives	12 black olives
1 tablespoonful fresh basil	1 tablespoonful fresh basil
Seasoning to taste	Seasoning to taste
¾ lb (350g) wholemeal vermicelli	2½ cupsful wholewheat vermicelli

1. Cut the pepper in half, remove the seeds, then place under a medium grill, skin side up, until it begins to colour. Cool slightly, then peel off the skin and slice the flesh into small pieces. Set aside.

2. Heat the oil in a pan and add the peeled and quartered garlic cloves. When they turn brown, remove and discard them. Peel and dice the aubergine (eggplant) and stir it into the oil, add the coarsely chopped tomatoes, and simmer for about 20 minutes, stirring often.

3. Now add the prepared pepper, chopped capers, halved olives (discard the stones) and the basil. Cover the pan and simmer for 10 minutes, stirring occasionally, by which time the sauce should be thick. Season well.

4. Meanwhile, cook the vermicelli in boiling water until just tender. Drain, then tip it onto a serving dish and cover with the sauce. Serve immediately.

CHICK PEAS AND PASTA

Ceci e pasta

Imperial (Metric)

½ lb (225g) chick peas
2 tablespoonsful vegetable oil
1 clove garlic, crushed
4 tomatoes
Parsley
Seasoning to taste
½ lb (225g) wholemeal spinach noodles
1 oz (25g) margarine or butter
Parsley to garnish

American

1 cupful garbanzo beans
2 tablespoonsful vegetable oil
1 clove garlic, crushed
4 tomatoes
Parsley
Seasoning to taste
1½ cupsful wholewheat spinach noodles
2½ tablespoonsful margarine or butter
Parsley to garnish

1. Soak the chick peas (garbanzo peas) overnight to speed up the cooking process. (You can use leftovers from a previous meal, or the tinned variety if you like.)

2. Heat the oil and *sauté* the garlic until it begins to colour. Add the drained chick peas (garbanzo beans), chopped tomatoes and parsley, plus just enough fresh water to cover the ingredients, cover the pan and simmer for about an hour, or until the chick peas (garbanzo beans) are tender. Add more water if necessary, and season towards the end of the cooking time.

3. When the chick peas (garbanzo beans) are almost ready, cook the noodles in boiling salted water. Drain them and stir into the other ingredients. Drain again to remove any excess liquid (the mixture should be fairly dry), and add the margarine. Serve at once.

TOMATOES STUFFED WITH PASTA

Pomodori ripieni di pasta

Imperial (Metric)	American
4 large tomatoes	4 large tomatoes
2 oz (50g) wholemeal spaghetti	2 ounces wholewheat spaghetti
1 tablespoonful fresh mint	1 tablespoonful fresh mint
1 tablespoonful parsley	1 tablespoonful parsley
2 tablespoonsful cooked lentils	2 tablespoonsful cooked lentils
Vegetable oil to mix	Vegetable oil to mix
Seasoning to taste	Seasoning to taste
Fresh mint to garnish	Fresh mint to garnish

1. Wash and dry the tomatoes, then cut a neat 'lid' off the top of each one, and scoop out the flesh. Stand the tomatoes upside down in a dish to drain, and set aside.

2. Break the spaghetti into small pieces and cook in boiling salted water for 5-10 minutes, or until just tender. Drain well. (Left-over pasta can also be used in this recipe.)

3. In a bowl combine a little of the tomato flesh — mashed to a pulp — with the pasta, chopped mint and parsley, and the lentils. Stir in just enough oil to moisten the mixture, and season to taste.

4. Arrange the tomatoes side by side in a small ovenproof dish and pack each one with some of the pasta and lentil mixture. Place the tomato lids back on top, and sprinkle with a few drops more of the oil.

5. Bake at 350°F/180°C (Gas Mark 4) for 15-20 minutes, or until the tomatoes are cooked. Serve hot or cold, garnished with sprigs of mint.

PASTA WITH BROCCOLI

Pasta e broccoli

Imperial (Metric)
1 lb (450g) fresh broccoli, or frozen equivalent
¾ lb (350g) wholemeal macaroni
3 tablespoonsful olive oil
1-2 cloves garlic, crushed
Seasoning to taste
1 oz (25g) roasted flaked almonds
Grated Parmesan cheese to serve (optional)

American
1 pound fresh broccoli, or frozen equivalent
3 cupsful wholewheat macaroni
3 tablespoonsful olive oil
1-2 cloves garlic, crushed
Seasoning to taste
¼ cupful roasted slivered almonds
Grated Parmesan cheese to serve (optional)

1. Trim the broccoli, cut into large florets, and put into a pan of boiling salted water.
2. Cook for 5 minutes, then add the macaroni to the water and continue cooking for 10 minutes, or until the broccoli and macaroni are both just tender. Drain and keep warm.
3. In a frying pan (skillet) heat the oil and *sauté* the crushed garlic until it begins to colour.
4. Stir in the broccoli and macaroni and heat through stirring frequently. If the mixture seems very dry, add a drop of the water in which the broccoli was cooked.
5. Season to taste and transfer to a serving dish, or individual plates. Sprinkle with the nuts. Hand cheese around at the table, if liked.

LASAGNE WITH PESTO SAUCE

Lasagne al pesto

Imperial (Metric)	American
½ lb (225g) wholemeal lasagne	½ pound wholewheat lasagne
Approx. 3 oz (75g) grated Parmesan cheese	Approx. ¾ cupful grated Parmesan cheese

Sauce:

Imperial (Metric)	American
1 bunch fresh basil leaves*	1 bunch fresh basil leaves*
1-2 cloves garlic, crushed	1-2 cloves garlic, crushed
1 oz (25g) pine nuts*	¼ cupful pine nuts*
2 oz (50g) grated Parmesan cheese	½ cupful grated Parmesan cheese
Seasoning to taste	Seasoning to taste
6-8 tablespoonsful olive oil	Approx. ½ cupful olive oil

1. Cook the lasagne in boiling salted water until just tender, then drain well, rinse in cold water, and set aside on a clean tea towel.
2. You can make the pesto sauce in a blender by combining all the ingredients except the oil, then adding it a few spoonsful at a time until the sauce is smooth and fairly thick. The traditional way to make it, however, is to grind the basil leaves, garlic, nuts, cheese and seasoning together in a mortar, and then to work in the oil until the sauce has the right consistency.
3. Alternate layers of the lasagne, cheese, and sauce in a shallow ovenproof dish. (If the sauce is too thick, add a drop of the water in which the lasagne was cooked.) Finish with an extra sprinkling of cheese. Bake at 400°F/200°C (Gas Mark 6) for 20 minutes.

*Although, to be authentic, pesto sauce should contain fresh basil leaves and pine nuts, it will still taste good if you substitute fresh parsley and walnuts.

LASAGNE WITH SPINACH

Lasagne agli spinaci

A delicious lasagne can also be made following the same method, and using the Ricotta and spinach filling given for Ravioli with Spinach (page 104). Spread this between the layers of cooked pasta, top with a tomato sauce and some Parmesan cheese. Bake at 400°F/200°C (Gas Mark 6) for about 30 minutes.

PASTA WITH PEAS AND MUSHROOMS

Tagliatelle con piselli e funghi

Imperial (Metric)
1½ oz (40g) margarine or butter
1 clove garlic, crushed
Parsley
Rosemary
¾ lb (350g) peas, fresh or frozen
½ lb (225g) mushrooms
Seasoning to taste
½ lb (225g) wholemeal tagliatelle
Grated cheese to serve (optional)

American
3½ tablespoonsful margarine or butter
1 clove garlic, crushed
Parsley
Rosemary
2 cupsful peas, fresh or frozen
4 cupsful mushrooms
Seasoning to taste
8 ounces wholewheat tagliatelle
Grated cheese to serve (optional)

1. Melt the margarine in a large frying pan (skillet), add the garlic, chopped parsley and a generous pinch of rosemary, and cook gently for 5 minutes.
2. Add the peas with just a drop of water (unless they are frozen, in which case there is no need for extra water), and simmer for 5 minutes.
3. Clean and slice the mushrooms before adding them, too, to the ingredients in the pan. Cook uncovered for a further 10 minutes, stirring occasionally, and adding more water if necessary. Season to taste.

4. At the same time as the sauce is cooking, plunge the tagliatelle into boiling salted water, then simmer for 10 minutes or until just cooked.
5. Drain the pasta, arrange it on a serving dish, and pour the peas and mushroom mixture over the top. Serve at once. Hand grated cheese around separately.

SPAGHETTI WITH RICOTTA SAUCE

Spaghetti con ricotta

This must be one of the easiest ways ever to prepare spaghetti!

Imperial (Metric)	**American**
10 oz (275g) wholemeal spaghetti	10 ounces wholewheat spaghetti
6 oz (175g) Ricotta cheese	3/4 cupful Ricotta cheese
2 oz (50g) grated Parmesan cheese	1/2 cupful grated Parmesan cheese
Good pinch of nutmeg	Good pinch of nutmeg
Seasoning to taste	Seasoning to taste
Fresh chives to garnish	Fresh chives to garnish

1. Plunge the spaghetti into boiling water and cook for 10 minutes, or until tender but still firm.
2. Meanwhile mash the Ricotta to make it creamy smooth, add the grated cheese, nutmeg, and seasoning to taste.
3. Drain the cooked spaghetti, put it into a bowl, and stir in the cheese mixture. Continue stirring until it has melted completely, then serve topped with a generous sprinkling of chopped chives.

RAVIOLI WITH SPINACH

Ravioli agli spinaci

Imperial (Metric)	American
½ lb (225g) wholemeal pasta dough (page 94)	8 ounces wholewheat pasta dough (page 94)
½ oz (12g) margarine or butter	1 tablespoonful margarine or butter
½ small onion	½ small onion
6 oz (175g) fresh spinach, or frozen equivalent	6 ounces fresh spinach, or frozen equivalent
6 oz (175g) Ricotta, curd or cream cheese	¾ cupful Ricotta, curd or cream cheese
2 oz (50g) grated Parmesan cheese	½ cupful grated Parmesan cheese
1 egg	1 egg
Pinch of grated nutmeg	Pinch of grated nutmeg
Seasoning to taste	Seasoning to taste

1. Roll out the dough on a lightly floured board, making it as thin as possible, then cut in half. Use a knife to mark one piece of the dough into squares about 2 in. (5cm) across.
2. Melt the margarine and fry the onion for a few minutes.
3. Cook the spinach, then drain very well, and chop finely.
4. In a bowl combine the onion, spinach, two cheeses and the well beaten egg. Add nutmeg and seasoning.
5. Place a teaspoonful of the filling in the centre of each of the marked squares of dough, then brush lightly along the lines with water.
6. Spread the other sheet of dough carefully over the first one, and use your fingers to press and seal along the water lines, making sure no air is trapped in the pockets.
7. Use a sharp knife or pastry cutter to cut the squares apart. Place the *ravioli* in a single layer on greaseproof paper or a floured tray, cover with a dampened cloth, and leave until you are ready to cook them.

8. Shortly before you wish to serve your *ravioli*, drop them a few at a time into a large pan of boiling salted water. Stir occasionally so that they do not stick together, and cook them for approximately 5-8 minutes, or until tender. Remove with a slotted spoon, drain thoroughly, and keep them warm whilst you cook the rest.

9. *Ravioli* can be served simply with a knob of butter, or with more Parmesan cheese, or maybe a spicy tomato sauce.

Note: Although most Italians fill their *ravioli* either with a cheese and spinach mixture such as this, or with meat, you can try filling them with a variety of ingredients including a thick lentil *purée*, béchamel sauce with chopped hard-boiled egg, and breadcrumbs with herbs and nuts.

SAVOURY BAKED MACARONI

Maccheroni al forno

Imperial (Metric)
1 oz (25g) margarine or butter
½ clove garlic, crushed
1 onion
1 small green pepper
½ lb (225g) tomatoes or tinned equivalent
4 oz (100g) mushrooms
Seasoning to taste
½ lb (225g) wholemeal macaroni
Approx. 4 oz (100g) grated cheese
10 black olives

American
2½ tablespoonsful margarine or butter
½ clove garlic, crushed
1 onion
1 small green pepper
8 ounces tomatoes or tinned equivalent
2 cupsful mushrooms
Seasoning to taste
2 cupsful wholewheat macaroni
Approx. 1 cupful grated cheese
10 black olives

1. Melt the margarine in a frying pan (skillet). Gently *sauté* the garlic for a few minutes, add the sliced onion and pepper, and continue cooking gently for 10 minutes, stirring now and again.

2. Peel and chop the tomatoes, and add to the pan with the sliced mushrooms; bring to the boil then cover and cook for 15 minutes more. Season to taste.

3. Meanwhile, cook the macaroni in boiling salted water for 10 minutes, or until tender, and drain thoroughly.

4. Put a third of the macaroni into a lightly greased ovenproof dish, cover with some of the sauce and then a sprinkling of cheese. Repeat this procedure twice. Arrange the olives over the top of the dish, plus a little extra cheese if liked.

5. Bake at 325°F/170°C (Gas Mark 3) for 15-20 minutes for the flavours to blend, and for all the ingredient to heat through. Serve at once.

8.
EGG AND CHEESE DISHES

Italians rely heavily on these two protein forms for use in dishes that do not contain meat or fish — possibly a little too heavily. At the same time they may not make full use of the wide variety available to them. Certain cheeses, for example, crop up in dish after dish, whilst many others that are still reasonably easy to obtain are served rarely, and then only at the end of the meal rather than as part of it.

If you cannot obtain any of the cheeses specified in the recipes here, substitute the varieties you *can* buy in your area. The results will be different, but should also be very edible.

Although the big cities in Italy are now selling more and more factory-farmed eggs, country folk know the value of keeping a few chickens — and the taste of really fresh, unadulterated eggs. Try to use only free-range in your kitchen. The flavour is better, the nutrients natural rather than synthetic, and the chickens that laid them for you will be living a better life.

Please note: an Italian *sformato* is very much like a soufflé, although it may not be quite as light. Often made in a mould, it holds its shape better — and has the added advantage of being less likely to go wrong. Italian omelettes may also turn out differently from those you are used to eating. Cooked longer and slower they tend to be more firm than our lighter, fluffier omelettes, and are usually served cut into wedges.

GREEN PEA SOUFFLÉ

Sformato di piselli

Imperial (Metric)

2 lb (1 kilo) green peas in shells, or frozen equivalent
1 oz (25g) margarine or butter
1 oz (25g) plain wholemeal flour
½ pint (275ml) milk
Seasoning to taste
4 eggs

American

2 pounds green peas in shells, or frozen equivalent
2½ tablespoonsful margarine or butter
4 tablespoonsful plain wholewheat flour
1¼ cupsful milk
Seasoning to taste
4 eggs

1. Shell the peas, and either boil or steam them for 10-15 minutes, or until soft. Drain them well, let cool slightly, then *purée* them in a blender.
2. Melt the margarine in a saucepan and sprinkle in the flour, cooking and stirring for a minute or two. Pour in the milk and continue cooking, stirring frequently, until the sauce thickens. Season well, then combine with the pea *purée*.
3. Separate the eggs and beat the yolks into the pea mixture. Whisk the egg whites until stiff and use a metal spoon to fold them carefully into the other ingredients.
4. Spoon them into a greased medium-sized soufflé dish. Bake at 350°F/180°C (Gas Mark 4) for about 30-40 minutes, or until set. Remove the dish from the oven and take to the table immediately.

Note: To serve this *sformato* in the Italian way, spoon the mixture into a well greased pudding basin, the top covered with silver foil, and stand it in a pan with a little hot water. Cook as above. When set, unmould the *sformato* onto a warm dish and serve at once. A tomato sauce would make a delicious accompaniment.

FENNEL AND CARROT SOUFFLÉ

Sformato di finocchi e carote

Imperial (Metric)	American
½ lb (225g) carrots	8 ounces carrots
4 fennel bulbs	4 fennel bulbs
Seasoning to taste	Seasoning to taste
2 oz (50g) grated Parmesan cheese	½ cupful grated Parmesan cheese
3 egg yolks	3 egg yolks
5 egg whites	5 egg whites

1. Slice the peeled carrots and boil or steam them until soft.
2. Trim, wash, and — in a separate pan — cook the fennel bulbs gently in boiling water for about 30 minutes, or until tender.
3. Drain both the vegetables and *purée* them in a blender. Mix well, and set aside to cool slightly.
4. When ready, add seasoning and grated cheese to the vegetable *purée*, then beat in the egg yolks.
5. Whisk the egg whites until stiff, and fold them into the first mixture.
6. Spoon into a greased medium-sized soufflé dish and bake at 375°F/190°C (Gas Mark 5) for 25-30 minutes, or until the *sformato* is puffed up and lightly browned. Serve immediately.

SAVOURY CHEESE RING

Ciambella al groviera

Imperial (Metric)
½ pint (275ml) water
4 oz (100g) margarine or butter
6 oz (175g) plain wholemeal flour
6 small eggs
6 oz (175g) Gruyère, or other hard cheese
Seasoning to taste

American
1¼ cupsful water
½ cupful margarine or butter
1½ cupsful plain wholewheat flour
6 small eggs
2 cupsful Gruyère, or other hard cheese
Seasoning to taste

1. Heat the water in a pan, then stir in the margarine until it has completely melted. When it boils, remove the pan from the heat and tip in all the flour at once, beating continually with a wooden spoon.
2. Carry on beating until the mixture comes away from the sides of the saucepan, then set aside to cool for a few minutes.
3. Add the eggs one at a time and beat well so that the mixture becomes smooth, and thick enough to hold its own shape (you may need to use only 5 eggs depending on their exact size).
4. Cut the cheese into small cubes, and stir most of it into the dough with the seasoning.
5. Grease a baking sheet and pipe or spoon the mixture into a wide ring (or use a large, shallow sandwich tin and pipe the mixture around its edge, leaving a space in the centre).
6. Dot the top of the ring with the rest of the cheese cubes. Bake at 300°F/150°C (Gas Mark 2) for 20 minutes, then at 350°F/180°C (Gas Mark 4) for 10-15 minutes more. This *ciambella* is served hot, cut in wedges, with a sauce such as béchamel, cheese or tomato. The amount given here should make 6 good portions.

SPAGHETTI OMELETTE

Frittata di spaghetti

Imperial (Metric)	**American**
10 oz (275g) wholemeal spaghetti	10 ounces wholewheat spaghetti
4 eggs	4 eggs
3 oz (75g) grated Parmesan cheese	¾ cupful grated Parmesan cheese
Handful of parsley	Handful of parsley
Seasoning to taste	Seasoning to taste
Pinch of nutmeg	Pinch of nutmeg
2 tablespoonsful vegetable oil	2 tablespoonsful vegetable oil

1. Cook the spaghetti in boiling water for 10 minutes, or until just tender. (You can use left-over spaghetti for this dish — which is probably how the Italians came to invent it!) Drain the spaghetti then put it into a bowl.
2. Add the beaten eggs, grated cheese, parsley, seasoning and nutmeg and mix well.
3. Heat the oil in a large frying pan (skillet) over a moderate heat. When it is hot, pour in the egg and spaghetti mixture, and distribute it evenly.
4. Cook gently, lifting the edges to allow the liquid to run underneath, until the eggs have set completely. If you like, you can finish this process by placing the omelette under the grill for a few minutes towards the end of the cooking time. Serve at once cut into wedges.

Note: This recipe is very flexible, and the balance of eggs and spaghetti varies from house to house — according, presumably, to what is in the larder. A less heavy version would, for example, be 6 ounces (175g) of spaghetti with 6 eggs. Any pasta can be used instead of the spaghetti.

ENDIVE OMELETTE

Frittata di indivia

It may seem a shame to cook this crisp curly lettuce, but its unusual flavour really does do something special for an omelette.

Imperial (Metric)	American
1 medium endive	1 medium endive
3 tablespoonsful vegetable oil	3 tablespoonsful vegetable oil
6 eggs	6 eggs
Seasoning to taste	Seasoning to taste
Chives to garnish	Chives to garnish

1. Trim the tough base of the stem, remove any wilted or damaged leaves, and wash the endive before shredding it coarsely. Steam for 5 minutes, then drain well and squeeze to make sure it is as dry as possible.
2. Heat the oil in a large frying pan (skillet) and cook the endive for a few minutes more, stirring frequently.
3. Beat the eggs with the seasoning and pour them over the endive, tipping the pan so that the mixture spreads evenly.
4. Continue cooking gently until the mixture begins to set, then flip the omelette over and cook the other side a few minutes more. (This is easiest to do if you hold a plate over the top of the pan, tip it so that the omelette rests on the plate and then slide it back into the pan.)
5. Serve piping hot, garnished with the chives, then cut into individual wedges.

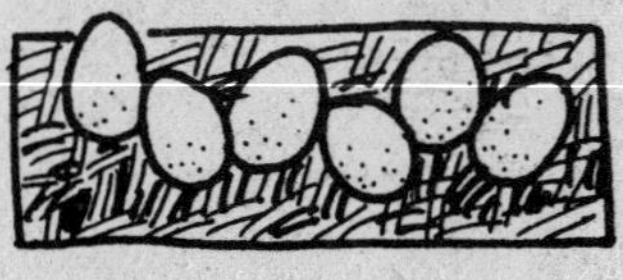

VEGETABLE OMELETTE

Frittata ortolano

Imperial (Metric)
3 tablespoonsful vegetable oil
1 carrot
2 sticks celery
2 small courgettes
1 small fennel bulb
2 oz (50g) mushrooms
4 eggs
Seasoning to taste

American
3 tablespoonsful vegetable oil
1 carrot
2 sticks celery
2 small zucchini
1 small fennel bulb
1 cupful mushrooms
4 eggs
Seasoning to taste

1. Heat the oil in a large ovenproof pan. Add the sliced carrot, celery sticks, courgettes (zucchini) and fennel bulb, and cook over a low heat for 5 minutes. Stir in the cleaned, sliced mushrooms and cook 5 minutes more.
2. Beat the eggs, season generously, and pour evenly over the vegetables in the pan.
3. Transfer it to the oven and bake at 350°F/180°C (Gas Mark 4) for 10-15 minutes, or until the eggs are set. If you prefer, cook your *frittata ortolano* on the top of your cooker, finishing it off by putting under the grill for a minute or two.
4. Serve hot, cut in thick wedges.

AUBERGINE BAKE

Torta di melanzane

Imperial (Metric)	**American**
2 medium aubergines	2 medium eggplants
Salt	Salt
Approx. 1 oz (25g) wholemeal flour	¼ cupful wholewheat flour
2 tablespoonsful vegetable oil	2 tablespoonsful vegetable oil
½ oz (12g) butter	1 tablespoonful butter
4 oz (100g) Mozzarella cheese	4 ounces Mozzarella cheese
4 eggs	4 eggs
Seasoning to taste	Seasoning to taste
Parsley	Parsley

1. Wash the aubergines (eggplants), then cut them lengthways into thin slices. Sprinkle with salt and lay them in a colander, cover, and leave to drain for at least 30 minutes. Rinse with cold water and pat dry before coating evenly with flour.
2. Heat the oil and butter together in a frying pan (skillet), and cook the slices until lightly browned on both sides. Drain on paper towels.
3. Lay half the slices across the base of an ovenproof dish, cover with slices of the Mozzarella cheese and top with the remainder of the aubergine (eggplant).
4. Beat together the eggs, seasoning, and chopped parsley, and pour the mixture carefully over the other ingredients. Bake at 350°F/180°C (Gas Mark 4) for 10-15 minutes, or until the eggs are set. Serve at once.

Note: Other vegetables can be used instead of aubergines (eggplants). Typically Italian recipes are made with courgettes (*torta di zucchini*), artichokes (*torta di carciofi*) and fennel (*torta di finnochi*).

LENTILS WITH EGGS

Lenticchie con uova

This is a particularly nice combination, and protein rich.

Imperial (Metric)	**American**
¾ lb (350g) brown lentils	1½ cupsful brown lentils
3 tablespoonsful olive oil	3 tablespoonsful olive oil
1 large onion	1 large onion
1 clove garlic, crushed	1 clove garlic, crushed
Seasoning to taste	Seasoning to taste
4 eggs	4 eggs
Sprigs of fresh mint to garnish	Sprigs of fresh mint to garnish

1. Wash the lentils carefully, then drain well.
2. Heat the oil in a frying pan (skillet) and, when warm, add the sliced onion and the garlic. Cook gently for 5-10 minutes until they begin to colour.
3. Stir in the lentils and seasoning, cover the pan, and cook gently for about an hour or until the lentils are soft and the liquid has been absorbed. (Take care that the mixture does not burn — if it seems too dry, add a drop of water or oil.)
4. Hard-boil the eggs shortly before you intend to serve the dish so that they are as hot as possible. Transfer the lentils to a serving dish, cut the eggs into quarters and arrange over the top of the lentils with sprigs of mint to garnish.

CHEESE AND ASPARAGUS SQUARES

Chizze di parmigiano agli asparagi

Pastry:

Imperial (Metric)	**American**
11 oz (300g) plain wholemeal flour	2¾ cupsful plain wholewheat flour
Pinch of salt	Pinch of salt
2 oz (50g) margarine or butter	5 tablespoonsful margarine or butter
2 egg yolks	2 egg yolks

Filling:

Imperial (Metric)	**American**
¾ lb (350g) asparagus spears, fresh, frozen or tinned	¾ pound asparagus spears, fresh, frozen or tinned
1 oz (25g) butter	2½ tablespoonsful butter
4 oz (100g) grated Parmesan cheese	1 cupful grated Parmesan cheese
Seasoning to taste	Seasoning to taste
1 egg white	1 egg white
Vegetable oil for frying	Vegetable oil for frying

1. Sift together the flour and salt, then rub in the margarine to make a mixture like fine breadcrumbs.
2. Stir in the lightly beaten egg yolks and knead to make a smooth dough — if necessary add a drop of lukewarm water. Cover and chill briefly.
3. Roll out the dough and use a knife or cutter (a tooth-edged is traditional) to cut an equal number of 2 in. (5cm) squares.
4. Cook the asparagus spears in water for just a few minutes, drain well, then *sauté* briefly in the butter. (If using the tinned variety, drain them then *sauté* — there is no need to cook them.) Drain on a paper towel.

5. Place a few of the spears on each of half the dough squares and sprinkle generously with cheese and seasoning. Brush the edges with the whisked egg white, cover with another square and press down firmly to seal.

6. Heat a deep pan of vegetable oil and fry the *chizze* a few at a time until golden — this should only take a few minutes. Drain them on paper towels and keep warm whilst you cook the rest. Serve hot.

RICOTTA FRITTERS

Frittelle di ricotta

Imperial (Metric)	**American**
3/4 pint (425ml) milk	2 cupsful milk
1/4 oz (7g) dried yeast	1/2 tablespoonful dried yeast
14 oz (400g) Ricotta cheese	1 3/4 cupsful Ricotta cheese
Approx. 2 oz (50g) plain wholemeal flour	Approx. 1/2 cupful plain wholewheat flour
Salt	Salt
Approx. 2 oz (50g) margarine or butter	5 tablespoonsful margarine or butter

1. Warm a drop of the milk, and stir in the yeast until it dissolves. Set aside.

2. In a separate bowl mash the Ricotta cheese, then add the rest of the milk. Sprinkle in enough flour to make the mixture smooth and paste-like. Add a pinch of salt, then the yeast, and combine gently but thoroughly.

3. Melt the margarine in a frying pan (skillet) and drop tablespoonsful of the cheese mixture to make small uneven fritters.

4. Fry for a minute or two until they begin to colour, then turn them over and fry the other side. Drain on paper towels and serve at once.

9.

SALADS

These can be served at any point during a meal — as a starter, an accompaniment to the main course, or to cleanse the mouth between dishes. Sometimes they are even served at the end of a meal to aid digestion, fennel being a particular favourite for this.

In general, Italian salads are not very imaginative. Despite the wide selection of vegetables, salads and fruits that are available, they tend to consist of a few basic ingredients, though it must be admitted that these are always fresh, crisp and attractively displayed. Herbs are used to add variety, as are wild plants and leaves found in the hedgerows, many of which are so strong and uniquely flavoured that only the tiniest amount is required. The dressing, usually a traditional one, will be made from the finest quality olive oil and a good wine vinegar. And rather than being reserved for dieters and hot summer days, salads are eaten — and enjoyed — by everyone in the family, every day of the year. This is an attitude, and a habit, that we would do well to cultivate!

For variety the Italian housewife may also add some cooked cold vegetables to her salad. Left-overs can be used up in this way and, providing the bulk of the salad is raw, will in no way detract from its nutritional value. She may also add some protein, although as the salad rarely forms the main dish of the meal, this is unlikely. Make more of a meal of your salad, if you wish, by adding beans, nuts, cheese, hard-boiled eggs, or a protein-rich dressing.

ITALIAN SALAD DRESSING

Imperial (Metric)	American
1 tablespoonful lemon juice	1 tablespoonful lemon juice
1 tablespoonful wine vinegar	1 tablespoonful wine vinegar
6 tablespoonsful olive oil	6 tablespoonsful olive oil
1 clove garlic, crushed	1 clove garlic, crushed
Seasoning to taste	Seasoning to taste

Combine the ingredients in a screw top jar, shake well to mix, then keep the dressing in the refrigerator to use as needed. If liked you can add some chopped fresh herbs — oregano goes especially well.

RAW MUSHROOM SALAD

Insalata di funghi crudi

Imperial (Metric)	American
½ lb (225g) small firm mushrooms	8 ounces small firm mushrooms
2-3 spring onions	2-3 scallions
2 teaspoonsful lemon juice	2 teaspoonsful lemon juice
3 tablespoonsful olive oil	3 tablespoonsful olive oil
Seasoning to taste	Seasoning to taste
Parsley to garnish	Parsley to garnish
Chicory to serve	Chicory to serve

1. Wash, pat dry, and cut the mushrooms into thick slices. Chop the onions as fine as possible.
2. In a bowl combine all the ingredients (except the chicory) gently but thoroughly, then cover and chill until needed.
3. Use the chicory leaves to line a small serving dish, then spoon the mushroom mixture into the centre and sprinkle generously with freshly chopped parsley.

CUCUMBER SALAD WITH CREAM AND CHEESE

Insalata di cetrioli alla panna e formaggio

Imperial (Metric)
1 large cucumber
½ small onion or 2 spring onions
½ clove garlic (optional)
2 tablespoonsful soured cream
Parsley
2 oz (50g) Fontina, Gruyère, or other hard cheese
Seasoning to taste

American
1 large cucumber
½ small onion or 2 scallions
½ clove garlic (optional)
2 tablespoonsful soured cream
Parsley
¾ cupful Fontina, Gruyère, or other hard cheese
Seasoning to taste

1. Peel and cut the cucumber into thick slices, then cut them into even sized chunks.
2. Chop the onion as fine as possible and crush the garlic. (For a more delicate flavour simply wipe the salad bowl with the cut garlic, then discard it.)
3. Mix together the cucumber, onion and garlic, cream, parsley, and diced cheese.
4. Season to taste and chill well before serving. This salad looks pretty garnished with extra parsley.

Note: For a very different salad using the same basic ingredients, replace the cream and parsley with plain yogurt and chopped nuts.

PEPPER SALAD

Insalata di peperoni

Imperial (Metric)	American
2 green peppers	2 green peppers
2 red peppers	2 red peppers
12 black olives	12 black olives

Dressing:

Imperial (Metric)	American
2 tablespoonsful red wine vinegar	2 tablespoonsful red wine vinegar
2 tablespoonsful vegetable oil, preferably olive	2 tablespoonsful vegetable oil, preferably olive
1 teaspoonful tomato *purée*	1 teaspoonful tomato paste
Soya sauce to taste	Soy sauce to taste
Pinch of paprika	Pinch of paprika
Seasoning to taste	Seasoning to taste

1. Top and tail the clean peppers, and cut into long strips. Put them in a pan and cover with cold water, then bring to the boil, and remove from heat almost at once. Drain and set peppers aside.
2. Whisk together all the ingredients for the dressing, and pour it over the peppers. Leave them to marinate for at least half an hour.
3. Stone and then chop the olives coarsely, and sprinkle over the salad before serving.

POTATO AND BROAD BEAN SALAD

Insalata di patate e fave

Imperial (Metric)	**American**
½ lb (225g) small potatoes	8 ounces small potatoes
½ lb (225g) fresh or frozen broad beans	8 ounces fresh or frozen Windsor beans
½ small onion	½ small onion
1 tablespoonful lemon juice	1 tablespoonful lemon juice
3 tablespoonsful olive oil	3 tablespoonsful olive oil
Parsley	Parsley
1 tablespoonful capers	1 tablespoonful capers
Seasoning to taste	Seasoning to taste

1. Scrub the potatoes, then steam them in their skins until just cooked — they should still be firm. Peel them if you like, then cut into cubes and put them into a bowl.
2. At the same time, cook the beans in boiling salted water for about 15 minutes, or until tender. Drain well, then mix with the potatoes.
3. Whilst the vegetables are still warm add the finely chopped onion, the lemon juice and oil, chopped parsley and capers, and seasoning to taste.
4. Chill well before serving garnished with extra parsley.

Note: If you can get hold of young fresh broad (Windsor) beans there is no need to cook them before adding them to the potatoes. Do as the southern Italians do, and eat them raw so you can enjoy their natural sweetness and crisp texture.

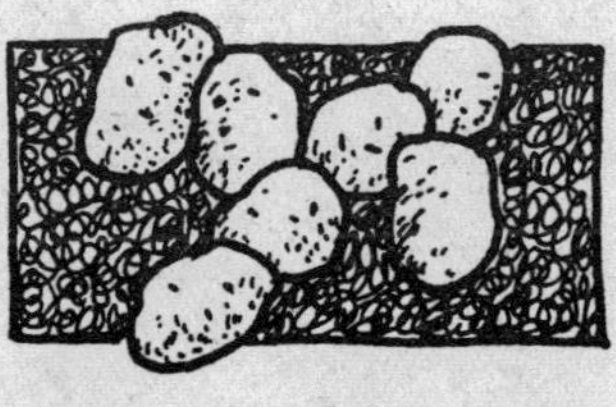

TOMATO SALAD WITH MOZZARELLA

Insalata di pomodori con Mozzarella

Imperial (Metric)	American
4 oz (100g) Mozzarella cheese	4 ounces Mozzarella cheese
1 lb (450g) firm tomatoes	1 pound firm tomatoes
1 cucumber	1 cucumber
10 pimento-stuffed olives	10 pimento-stuffed olives
Italian salad dressing (page 119)	Italian salad dressing (page 119)
Fresh chives to garnish	Fresh chives to garnish

1. Cut the cheese into fairly thick slices, the tomatoes and cucumber into thinner slices.
2. Arrange them in circles on a serving dish, alternating them for colour contrast, and overlapping them slightly. Sprinkle with the chopped olives.
3. Pour just a little drop of dressing over the salad, and garnish with the chives. Put the dressing on the table so that anyone who wants more can help themselves.

DANDELION SALAD

Insalata di campagnola

Dandelion leaves, rarely eaten in this country, are still very popular in much of Italy. Like most green leaves they are a good source of minerals and vitamins.

Imperial (Metric)	American
1½ lb (¾ kilo) dandelion leaves	1½ pounds dandelion leaves
Italian salad dressing (page 119)	Italian salad dressing (page 119)
3 eggs or soya 'bacon' bits	3 eggs or soya 'bacon' bits

1. The leaves should be fresh picked, preferably early in the day, and from ground that is not close to a road. Young leaves are by far the tastiest.
2. Wash the dandelion leaves thoroughly, pat dry, then trim any tough stems or damaged leaves. Shred coarsely and place in a serving bowl. Add a small amount of salad dressing, toss well, and chill briefly.
3. If using eggs, hard boil them first, then cool completely. Serve the salad scattered with the chopped eggs or do as many Italians do, and add crisp 'bacon' bits to contrast with the fresh green leaves.

CAULIFLOWER SALAD

Insalata di cavolfiore

Imperial (Metric)
1 medium cauliflower
1 yellow pepper
2 tomatoes
10 black olives
2 tablespoonsful mayonnaise
2 tablespoonsful plain yogurt
Pinch of dry mustard
Seasoning to taste

American
1 medium cauliflower
1 yellow pepper
2 tomatoes
10 black olives
2 tablespoonsful mayonnaise
2 tablespoonsful plain yogurt
Pinch of dry mustard
Seasoning to taste

1. Clean the cauliflower, then break it into florets. Bring a saucepan of salted water to the boil and cook the cauliflower for 3-4 minutes. Drain, plunge at once into cold water, then drain well again.
2. Tip the cauliflower florets into a serving bowl. Add the sliced pepper, quartered tomatoes and olives.
3. Mix together the mayonnaise, yogurt, mustard and seasoning. Use just enough of the dressing to lightly coat the salad ingredients. Chill well before serving.

Note: Although Italians usually cook their cauliflower before using it in a recipe such as this, a young crisp cauliflower can be delicious if used in the same combination, but left raw.

MIXED SALAD

Insalata mista

In an Italian mixed salad, anything goes! This is just one suggested combination, but you can use whatever ingredients you have handy.

Imperial (Metric)	American
1 clove garlic	1 clove garlic
1 small crisp lettuce	1 small crisp lettuce
1 small endive	1 small endive
8 radishes	8 radishes
½ green pepper	½ green pepper
2 tomatoes	2 tomatoes
2 sticks celery	2 sticks celery
½ small fennel bulb	½ small fennel bulb
8 green olives	8 green olives
Italian salad dressing (page 119)	Italian salad dressing (page 119)

1. Cut the garlic clove and use it to wipe around the inside of the salad bowl, then discard it.
2. Wash and shred the lettuce, wash and separate the endive leaves (the contrast between pale and dark is what is important here).
3. Slice the radishes, pepper, tomatoes and celery sticks. Cut the fennel into thin slivers.
4. Use the two lettuces to make a base in your serving bowl then mix the remaining ingredients and spoon them into the centre.
5. Add just enough dressing to coat the ingredients lightly, yet leave none in the bottom of the bowl. Serve at once, with more dressing on the table for those who want it.

KIDNEY BEAN SALAD

Insalata di fagioli

Imperial (Metric)
½ lb (225g) kidney beans, soaked overnight
3 spring onions
4 tablespoonsful wine vinegar
3 tablespoonsful olive oil
2-3 sticks celery
Seasoning to taste
Lettuce to serve

American
1¼ cupsful kidney beans, soaked overnight
3 scallions
⅓ cupful wine vinegar
3 tablespoonsful olive oil
2-3 sticks celery
Seasoning to taste
Lettuce to serve

1. Bring a saucepan of water to the boil, add the kidney beans and boil for 10 minutes, then simmer the kidney beans for about an hour, or until tender. Drain and set aside to cool. (You could save time by using pre-cooked beans left over from another meal, or tinned beans.)
2. Chop the onions and put them into a screw top jar with the wine vinegar and oil. Shake well.
3. Chop the celery sticks into small pieces and combine them with the beans, then add the dressing and stir. Season to taste. Chill for a short time if possible for the flavours to blend.
4. Serve the bean mixture on a bed of crisp pale lettuce.

Note: Other beans can be used in this recipe, or even a combination of different varieties. Italians are especially fond of chick peas (garbanzo beans) and haricot (navy) beans, and often serve them together with cold, cooked green beans. They sometimes add hard-boiled eggs to their salad too.

FENNEL AND ORANGE SALAD

Insalata di finocchi con arancia

Imperial (Metric)	American
1 large fennel bulb	1 large fennel bulb
½ cucumber	½ cucumber
½ red pepper	½ red pepper
1 large orange	1 large orange
2 tablespoonsful olive oil	2 tablespoonsful olive oil
1 tablespoonful lemon juice	1 tablespoonful lemon juice
1-2 teaspoonsful fresh mint	1-2 teaspoonsful fresh mint
Seasoning to taste	Seasoning to taste
4 oz (100g) hard cheese	1 cupful hard cheese
2 oz (50g) walnuts	½ cupful English walnuts

1. Trim the coarse outer leaves and base of the fennel, then cut it downwards into thin slices. Dice the cucumber, slice the pepper. Peel the orange and divide into segments.
2. In a screw top jar, mix together the oil, lemon juice, finely chopped mint and seasoning. Shake well.
3. In a serving bowl combine the fennel, cucumber and pepper, and toss in the salad dressing.
4. Cut the cheese into cubes, and stir it into the other ingredients together with the walnuts and orange segments. Serve immediately, with extra dressing available for those who want it.

10.

SWEETS AND SWEET THINGS

In general, Italians do not have a very sweet tooth. The most popular dessert is fruit followed by cheese — and the fruit will be fresh and unadorned, even strawberries being topped with a squeeze of orange or lemon juice rather than cream and sugar! However, there are a few favourites that crop up at weekends and on special occasions. Ice-cream is one of them, although this tends to be eaten on the streets and beaches more often than it is served at the meal table. Cheesecake, the traditional and rather plain variety, is another popular dessert dish, as are all fruit flans. Chestnuts, whole or mashed, soaked in wine or covered with cream, feature on every restaurant menu. Fresh fruit salad is given a real flip by the addition of liqueurs, making it the ideal end-of-meal choice — light, fresh tasting, and great for the digestion. In fact, the Italians use liqueurs in many of their desserts, as you will note in the recipes that follow. They have been included firstly to make the recipes authentic, and secondly because they do make a subtle but superb difference to dessert dishes that could be rather ordinary without them. If, however, you prefer not to use alcohol, just leave it out — you could add a drop of fruit juice to take its place.

Another ingredient that features often in Italian desserts and baked goods is candied peel. You can, of course, buy this ready made, but it will contain sugar, preservatives, and possibly colouring. If you are concerned about eating for health, either replace it with a little freshly grated orange or lemon rind, or with chopped dried fruit. Another alternative is to make your own candied peel at home using raw cane sugar.

RICOTTA AND COFFEE DESSERT

Ricotta al caffe

Imperial (Metric)	**American**
½ lb (225g) Ricotta cheese	1 cupful Ricotta cheese
4 oz (100g) raw cane sugar, powdered in grinder	½ cupful raw cane sugar, powdered in grinder
2 tablespoonsful rum	2 tablespoonsful rum
3 tablespoonsful freshly roasted ground coffee	3 tablespoonsful freshly roasted ground coffee
Whipped cream to serve (optional)	Whipped cream to serve (optional)

1. Put the Ricotta cheese into a bowl and use a wooden spoon to mash it until it has the consistency of a thick cream.
2. Stir in the sugar and rum, distributing them evenly through the cheese.
3. Add the coffee (this must be very finely ground or the texture will be gritty). When well mixed, chill the cheese for a few hours.
4. Serve in individual glasses. *Ricotta al caffe* is delicious topped with just a spoonful of whipped cream.

CHEESE STUFFED PEARS

Pere ripiene

Imperial (Metric)	American
4 ripe pears	4 ripe pears
1-2 teaspoonsful lemon juice	1-2 teaspoonsful lemon juice
2 oz (50g) Gorgonzola, or other blue cheese	½ cupful Gorgonzola, or other blue cheese
1 oz (25g) unsalted butter	2½ tablespoonsful unsalted butter
2 oz (50g) walnuts	½ cupful English walnuts

1. Halve the pears lengthways and, if the skins seem tough or blemished, peel them. Brush the cut surfaces lightly with lemon juice. Use a sharp spoon or small knife to remove the cores and a little of the flesh to leave a hollow.
2. Cream together the cheese and butter until light and well blended, then use the mixture to fill each of the pear halves.
3. Press them together again firmly so that you have four whole pears, and roll these in the coarsely crushed walnuts.
4. Arrange them attractively on a small serving dish and chill for an hour or two before serving.

MELON WATER ICE

Granita di melone

Imperial (Metric)	**American**
1 large ogen melon	1 large ogen melon
4 oz (100g) raw cane sugar	½ cupful raw cane sugar
¼ pint (150ml) water	⅔ cupful water
1 teaspoonful lemon juice	1 teaspoonful lemon juice
Stem ginger preserved in honey (optional)	Stem ginger preserved in honey (optional)

1. Peel, seed, and coarsely chop the melon before *puréeing* the flesh in a blender, or pushing it through a sieve.
2. Combine the sugar and water in a saucepan, heat gently and stir until the sugar dissolves. Raise the heat and boil the mixture for 4-5 minutes more, without stirring, then set aside to cool.
3. Add the syrup to the melon *purée*, stir in the lemon juice, and pour the mixture into a shallow freezing tray. Set the freezer on a high temperature, and leave the mixture until it begins to firm up. Whip lightly to add air and improve the texture. Re-freeze.
4. Serve your *granita di melone* in chilled glasses. A few pieces of stem ginger, and a spoonful of the liquid in which they were preserved, make a perfect topping.

Note: This basic recipe can be used to turn most fruits into water ices — the Italians are particularly fond of *granita di fragole* (strawberry water ice), *granita di lamponi* (raspberry water ice); and *granita di limone* and *arance* (lemon and orange water ices), both made with concentrated juices rather than fruit *purées*.

MONT BLANC (CHESTNUTS AND CREAM)

Monte Bianco

Imperial (Metric)	American
1 lb (450g) fresh chestnuts or equivalent from a tin	1 pound fresh chestnuts or equivalent from a tin
½ lb (225g) raw cane sugar	1 cupful raw cane sugar
¼ pint (150ml) whipping cream	⅔ cupful heavy cream
1 tablespoonful brandy (optional)	1 tablespoonful brandy (optional)

1. Put the fresh chestnuts into a saucepan, cover them with water, and boil for 10 minutes. Cool slightly, then carefully remove the outer shell and inner skin. Cover with fresh water and continue cooking for 20-30 minutes, or until soft. Tinned chestnuts should not need to be cooked first.
2. Drain the chestnuts, then *purée* in a blender and tip into a bowl. Stir in the sugar whilst the chestnut *purée* is still warm so it will dissolve. (To make sure it is especially smooth you can, if liked, powder the sugar in a grinder first.)
3. Adjust the amount of sugar to make the mixture firm enough to hold a shape, then mould it into four cone shapes.
4. Decorate the top of each one with some whipped cream — it is traditional to add a little brandy, but not absolutely necessary. This simple yet rather special dessert is best made shortly before you intend to serve it.

CHOCOLATE TRUFFLES

Tartufi al cioccolato

Imperial (Metric)
4 oz (100g) bitter chocolate (preferably made with raw sugar)
1 tablespoonful milk
1½ oz (40g) butter
1 egg yolk
1 oz (25g) cocoa or carob powder

American
4 ounces bitter chocolate (preferably made with raw sugar)
1 tablespoonful milk
3½ tablespoonsful butter
1 egg yolk
¼ cupful cocoa or carob powder

1. In a double boiler, or a heavy-based saucepan, gently melt the chocolate in the milk.
2. When completely dissolved blend in the butter, remove from the heat and add the egg yolk, mixing well.
3. Chill for a few hours so that the mixture firms up, then shape into small balls.
4. Roll each one in the cocoa to coat it completely, then chill again until needed. They should be eaten within 2 days.

Note: For a healthier sweet, you can use a carob 'chocolate' bar instead of the bitter chocolate — just follow the same instructions.

CHEESECAKE

Torta di ricotta

Pastry:

Imperial (Metric)	American
½ lb (225g) plain wholemeal flour	2 cupsful plain wholewheat flour
Pinch of salt	Pinch of salt
6 oz (175g) margarine or butter	¾ cupful margarine or butter
2 egg yolks	2 egg yolks
1 teaspoonful grated lemon peel	1 teaspoonful grated lemon peel
Cold water to mix	Cold water to mix

Filling:

Imperial (Metric)	American
1 lb (450g) Ricotta cheese	2 cupsful Ricotta cheese
1 oz (25g) plain wholemeal flour	4 tablespoonsful plain wholewheat flour
1 tablespoonful grated orange peel	1 tablespoonful grated orange peel
1 tablespoonful grated lemon peel	1 tablespoonful grated lemon peel
2 tablespoonsful sultanas	2 tablespoonsful golden seedless raisins
Vanilla essence	Vanilla essence
4 oz (100g) raw cane sugar, powdered in grinder	½ cupful raw cane sugar, powdered in grinder
3 eggs	3 eggs
1 oz (25g) flaked almonds	¼ cupful slivered almonds

1. Sift together the flour and salt, then rub in the margarine to make a crumb-like mixture.

2. Beat the egg yolks lightly and mix into the flour and margarine, sprinkle in the lemon peel, and add just enough cold water to bind the ingredients together. Knead briefly then cover and chill.

3. Combine the cheese and sifted flour, blending them well so that the mixture is smooth. Stir in the grated peel, sultanas, a drop of vanilla essence, and lastly the sugar.

4. Beat the eggs until they begin to foam, and stir into the other ingredients.

5. Roll out the pastry and use to line an 8 in. (20cm) loose bottomed flan dish, or ring standing on a baking sheet. Pour in the filling, spreading it evenly, then scatter the almonds over the top. (Any extra pastry can be used to make a decorative lattice pattern.)

6. Bake at 350°F/180°C (Gas Mark 4) for 50 minutes to an hour, or until the filling is firm and the pastry cooked. Cool slightly, then transfer carefully to a wire rack and leave to get completely cold. This rich cheesecake is especially good served with a fresh fruit — white grapes often acompany it in Italy.

Note: If you cannot obtain Ricotta cheese, try this recipe using curd cheese, or sieved cottage cheese with a few spoonsful of cream added. And those with a sweeter tooth might prefer using chopped candied peel in the filling rather than the sharper tasting fresh orange and lemon.

APPLE FRITTERS

Frittelle di mele

Batter:

Imperial (Metric)	American
1 teaspoonful dried yeast	1 teaspoonful dried yeast
2 teaspoonsful warm water	2 teaspoonsful warm water
2 oz (50g) plain wholemeal flour	½ cupful plain wholewheat flour
1 oz 625g) raw cane sugar	2 tablespoonsful raw cane sugar
3 eggs	3 eggs
2 oz (50g) melted butter	5 tablespoonsful melted butter
¼ pint (150ml) milk	⅔ cupful milk

Filling:

Imperial (Metric)	American
6 firm dessert apples	6 firm dessert apples
1 oz (25g) raw cane sugar, powdered in grinder	2 tablespoonsful raw cane sugar, powdered in grinder
Vegetable oil for frying	Vegetable oil for frying

1. Mix the yeast with the warm water until it dissolves, then set aside to become frothy.
2. Put the flour in a bowl, add the sugar, beaten eggs, melted butter and milk.
3. When ready, add the yeast to the other ingredients and beat so that the batter is completely smooth.
4. Peel and core the apples, then cut into even-sized rings. Sprinkle with the powdered sugar to help the batter stick.
5. Heat the oil in a deep fryer. Dip the apple rings into the batter a few at a time, then drop into the hot oil and cook for a few minutes, or until the outsides are lightly browned and crisp. Drain on paper towels, and serve hot.

STRAWBERRY ICE CREAM

Gelato alle fragole

Imperial (Metric)	**American**
1 lb (450g) ripe strawberries	1 pound ripe strawberries
1 tablespoonful lemon juice	1 tablespoonful lemon juice
1 tablespoonful orange juice	1 tablespoonful orange juice
3 oz (75g) raw cane sugar, powdered in grinder	½ cupful raw cane sugar, powdered in grinder
½ pint (275ml) whipping cream	1¼ cupsful heavy cream

1. Make a *purée* of the strawberries by either putting them into a blender or rubbing through a sieve.
2. Drain off any excess liquid, then stir in the lemon and orange juice, plus the sugar.
3. Whip the cream lightly until it can just hold its shape, then fold it into the fruit *purée*.
4. Turn the mixture into a freezing tray, cover, and freeze until set firm. Serve in chilled glasses.

APRICOT ICE CREAM

Gelato alle albicocche

Can be made in the same way as *gelato di fragole*, but using one pound of fresh apricots for the *purée* instead of the strawberries. The Italians often use eggs in their ice-creams — add 2 or 3 egg yolks to the apricot *purée* before the whipped cream is folded in for an especially rich tasting, smooth textured *gelato di albicocche*.

PINE NUT SWEETS

Pinoccate

Imperial (Metric)	American
5 oz (130g) pine nuts	1 cupful pine nuts
¾ lb (350g) raw cane sugar	2 cupsful raw cane sugar
¼ pint (150ml) water	⅔ cupful water
2 tablespoonsful grated lemon peel	2 tablespoonsful grated lemon peel

1. Cook the pine nuts in a medium oven for a few minutes, but do not let them colour. Set aside to cool.
2. In a heavy-based saucepan combine the sugar and water, stir well, then cook slowly until the sugar dissolves. Bring the mixture to the boil and continue cooking until the syrup reaches hard crack stage. You can test this by dropping a spoonful of the mixture into a cup of cold water — when it separates into firm threads it is ready.
3. Remove from the heat at once and stir in the nuts and grated lemon peel. Spoon or drop into small uneven heaps on a baking sheet covered with greased foil, and leave to cool completely. Store in an airtight jar or tin. Makes approximately 20.

Note: Pinoccate are made in various parts of Italy, each area having its own version (and spelling!). Some add chopped bitter chocolate instead of the lemon, others use candied orange peel, often soaking it first in a drop of Maraschino liqueur.

SICILIAN CAKE

Cassata Siciliana

Traditionally this was prepared at Easter only, but now it turns up regularly on high days and holidays. Surprisingly, it is very easy to put together, especially if the sponge is made in advance.

Sponge:

Imperial (Metric)	**American**
2 eggs	2 eggs
2 oz (50g) raw cane sugar, powdered in grinder	4 tablespoonsful raw cane sugar, powdered in grinder
Vanilla essence	Vanilla essence
2 oz (50g) self-raising wholemeal flour	½ cupful self-raising wholewheat flour

Filling:

Imperial (Metric)	**American**
1 lb (450g) Ricotta or curd cheese	2 cupsful Ricotta or curd cheese
6 oz (175g) raw cane sugar, powdered in grinder	¾ cupful raw cane sugar, powdered in grinder
3-4 tablespoonsful Maraschino, Cointreau or Grand Marnier liqueur	⅓ cupful Maraschino, Cointreau or Grand Marnier liqueur
1 oz (25g) pistachio nuts or almonds	¼ cupful pistachio nuts or almonds
3 oz (75g) candied peel	½ cupful candied peel
2 oz (50g) bitter chocolate	2 ounces bitter chocolate

1. To make the sponge, whisk together the eggs and sugar until the mixture thickens. Stir in the vanilla essence.

2. Sieve the flour to make sure there are no lumps, then fold it into the eggs and sugar. If the eggs are small and the mixture rather dry, add a tiny drop of hot water.

3. Spoon into a small lined and greased loaf tin, and bake at 350°F/180°C (Gas Mark 4) for 20-25 minutes, or until you can press a finger firmly on the top of the cake, and leave no impression.
4. Turn out carefully and stand on a wire rack to cool.
5. Sieve the cheese, then beat it together with the sugar and liqueur. Chop the nuts, candied peel and chocolate into small pieces, and stir them into the mixture.
6. When the sponge is cold, cut it crossways into three long oblong strips about ½ in. (13mm) thick. Lay the first one on a flat plate and spread it with half the cheese mixture. Top with another sponge slice, then the rest of the cheese. Add the final slice of sponge and press down firmly.
7. Cover the *cassata* with foil and chill well, for at least two hours; before serving cut into thick slices. It is best taken from the fridge just before it is needed.

Note: If you want your *cassata* to look more impressive, you can decorate it in a number of ways. The simplest is to divide the ingredients for the filling in two before you add the nuts, peel and chocolate. Proceed as above with one half of the cheese, and shortly before serving the *cassata* use the second half to make an icing over the top and sides of the sponge block. This can be decorated with grated chocolate, glacé cherries, chopped peel, more nuts — whatever takes your fancy.

Alternatively, make a chocolate icing and cover the *cassata* with this, decorating it with candied fruit slices and glace cherries, or by piping extra chocolate icing into patterns on top of the cake.

11.
CAKES, BISCUITS AND OTHER BAKED GOODS

Every Italian village, however small, has its own *pasticceria*, its counter crammed with a variety of tiny biscuits, rather plain cakes, and with large and small fruit tarts adding splashes of bright colour to the whole display. If home baking has declined in popularity, the art of the Italian pastry cook — renowned for many centuries — is as much appreciated now as ever it was. Fresh baked goodies delivered every morning do not stay around long enough to go stale!

Many of the items you will see at the bakers are, however, quite easy to make at home. And most of the ingredients used in Italian cakes and biscuits are healthy ones — nuts, dried fruits, honey. You can make them more so by substituting wholemeal flour for white, raw cane sugar for refined. If you want them to look as light as the originals would, use 81 per cent wholemeal flour and the paler variety of raw sugar.

Another healthy idea — Italians use Ricotta cheese to take the place of cream in their tarts and flans. As it is virtually fat-free, and as low in calories as cottage cheese, it makes an ideal substitute.

JAM TURNOVERS

Bocconcini alla marmellata

Pastry:

Imperial (Metric)	**American**
$\frac{1}{2}$ lb (225g) plain wholemeal flour	2 cupsful plain wholewheat flour
$\frac{1}{2}$ oz (12g) raw cane sugar	1 tablespoonful raw cane sugar
Pinch of salt	Pinch of salt
3 tablespoonsful vegetable oil	3 tablespoonsful vegetable oil
$\frac{1}{4}$ pint (150ml) white wine	$\frac{2}{3}$ cupful white wine

Filling:

Imperial (Metric)	**American**
Approx. 4 oz (100g) raw sugar jam	Approx. 4 tablespoonsful raw sugar jelly
1 oz (25g) flaked almonds	$\frac{1}{4}$ cupful slivered almonds
Vegetable oil for frying	Vegetable oil for frying

1. Sift the flour and stir in the sugar and salt. Add the oil and wine to make a soft dough. Chill, if possible, for a short time before rolling out very thin, then cutting into circles with a cutter or medium-sized cup.
2. Spoon some jam onto one side of each of the circles and sprinkle with a few nuts. Fold the other side of the dough over the jam to make a small half moon, and dampen the edges before pressing them firmly together.
3. Set aside for a short while then deep fry the turnovers, a few at a time, in the hot oil. As they change colour and the pastry becomes firm, remove them at once and drain on paper towels. They can be served warm or cold.

Note: Although these are traditionally fried in oil, *bocconcini* can also be baked in the oven to make a more English-style jam turnover.

GRAPE TARTS

Pasticcini all'uva

Pastry:

Imperial (Metric)	American
½ lb (225g) plain wholemeal flour	2 cupsful plain wholewheat flour
4 oz (100g) margarine or butter	½ cupful margarine or butter
Cold water to mix	Cold water to mix

Filling:

Imperial (Metric)	American
5 oz (130g) white grapes	5 ounces white grapes
5 oz (130g) black grapes	5 ounces black grapes
½ lb (225g) Ricotta or cream cheese	1 cupful Ricotta or cream cheese
1 tablespoonful liqueur (optional)	1 tablespoonful liqueur (optional)
2 oz (50g) raw cane sugar, powdered in grinder	¼ cupful raw cane sugar, powdered in grinder

1. Sift the flour into a bowl and use your fingertips to rub in the margarine. When the mixture is like fine crumbs, add cold water, a few drops at a time, and knead until you have a smooth, pliable dough. Wrap in aluminium foil or clingfilm and set aside to chill for at least 30 minutes.
2. Roll out the pastry and use a cutter or cup to make approximately 12 small circles. Arrange these in lightly greased tart tins, prick with a fork, and bake at 375°F/190°C (Gas Mark 5) for 10 minutes, or until the pastry is cooked. Set aside to cool before removing carefully from the tins.
3. Wash and dry the grapes.
4. Use a wooden spoon to mash the cheese together with the liqueur until it is soft and completely smooth. Mix in the sugar, then stir in most of the grapes.

5. Pile a little of the mixture into each of the tart shells and use the left-over grapes as decoration. Serve your *piccole torte* as soon as possible after preparing them.

NUT CAKE

Torta di noci

Imperial (Metric)	American
4 oz (100g) margarine or butter	1/2 cupful margarine or butter
4 oz (100g) self-raising wholemeal flour	1 cupful self-raising wholewheat flour
5 oz (130g) raw cane sugar	2/3 cupful raw cane sugar
2 eggs	2 eggs
1 tablespoonful grated lemon peel	1 tablespoonful grated lemon peel
1/2 lb (225g) mixed nuts	1 1/2 cupsful mixed nuts
1 oz (25g) walnuts	1/4 cupful English walnuts

1. Use a little of the margarine to grease an 8 in. (20cm) cake tin, then dust lightly with some of the flour, shaking off the excess.
2. Beat the rest of the margarine with the sugar until creamy, add the lightly whisked eggs and peel, and beat a few minutes more.
3. Grind or chop the nuts very fine and mix them with the flour.
4. Fold the dry ingredients into the first mixture, making sure everything is well blended, then spoon it into the prepared tin and smooth the top.
5. Bake at 350°F/180°C (Gas Mark 4) for 50 minutes to an hour, or until the cake is just firm to touch. Cool for a short time before turning it out of the tin, and standing on a wire rack to get completely cold. Wrap your *torta di noci* in foil if you intend to keep it a day or two.

FRUIT AND NUT TURNOVERS

Nepitelle

Pastry:

Imperial (Metric)	American
½ lb (225g) plain wholemeal flour	2 cupsful plain wholewheat flour
Pinch of salt	Pinch of salt
4 oz (100g) margarine or butter	½ cupful margarine or butter
3 oz (75g) raw cane sugar, powdered in grinder	½ cupful raw cane sugar, powdered in grinder
2 egg yolks	2 eggs yolks

Filling:

Imperial (Metric)	American
6 oz (175g) dried figs	1¼ cupsful dried figs
4 oz (100g) raisins	¾ cupful raisins
3 oz (75g) roasted almonds	¾ cupful roasted almonds
3 oz (75g) walnuts	¾ cupful English walnuts
2 tablespoonsful grated orange peel	2 tablespoonsful grated orange peel
Pinch of ground cloves	Pinch of ground cloves
1 teaspoonful mixed spice	1 teaspoonful mixed spice
Approx. 4 tablespoonsful clear honey	Approx. ⅓ cupful clear honey
1 egg white	1 egg white

1. Sift together the flour and salt, then use fingertips to rub in the margarine to form a mixture like fine crumbs. Stir in the sugar, then the egg yolks so you have a soft dough, and knead briefly. Cover the dough and chill.

2. Wash the dried fruit then plump up in hot water. Drain, pat dry, and chop into small pieces. Either grind or chop the nuts as fine as possible. In a bowl mix together the fruit, nuts, peel, spices, and add enough honey to moisten the mixture.

3. Roll out the dough and cut into small circles with a cutter or cup.

4. Divide the fruit and nut mixture between the circles, putting it on one half only. Dampen the edges of the dough with a little of the egg white, fold to form a half-moon, and press the edges to seal.

5. Brush the tops with more egg white, and prick or cut them to let air escape. Arrange on a lightly greased baking sheet.

6. Cook your *nepitelle* in a medium oven, 350°F/180°C (Gas Mark 4) for 20-30 minutes, or until the pastry is done. Delicious served hot, warm or cold.

FRIED PASTRY KNOTS

Cenci

These are an ideal nibble to serve with pre-dinner drinks, or to put on a buffet table. Children enjoy them too — and they're certainly better for them than sweets!

Imperial (Metric)	American
4 oz (100g) plain 81 per cent wholemeal flour*	1 cupful plain 81 per cent wholewheat flour*
½ oz (12g) butter	1 tablespoonful butter
Pinch of salt	Pinch of salt
1½ oz (40g) raw cane sugar, powdered in grinder	3 tablespoonsful raw cane sugar, powdered in grinder
1 egg	1 egg
½ tablespoonful brandy or rum (optional)	½ tablespoonful brandy or rum (optional)
Vegetable oil for frying	Vegetable oil for frying

1. Sift the flour into a bowl with the salt, and rub in the butter, then stir in ½ ounce (12g) of the sugar.
2. Add the egg and alcohol, and knead the mixture well to make a stiff paste (if not using alcohol you may need to use a large egg, or add a little extra liquid by using part of another one). Cover the dough and let rest for at least 15 minutes.
3. Divide the dough into two or three and roll out each piece on a floured board until it is as thin as you can possibly make it. Use a pastry cutter or sharp knife to cut small oblong strips about ½ in. (13mm) wide, and tie these into a simple knot.
4. Heat some vegetable oil in a pan, and drop in the pieces of dough a few at a time. Cook for 1-2 minutes, until crisp and brown, then scoop out with a slotted spoon. Drain on paper towels and continue to cook the rest of the *cenci*.

5. When they have cooled slightly, sprinkle them with the remaining sugar. They can be stored for a short time if left covered in a dry place, or in a tin, but are really best if eaten shortly after they are made.

*Although you could use 100 per cent wholemeal flour if you prefer, the coarseness of the bran prevents these pastry knots from having the very light, fine texture of the authentic Italian *cenci*. It also makes it difficult to roll the pastry out as paper thin as is necessary.

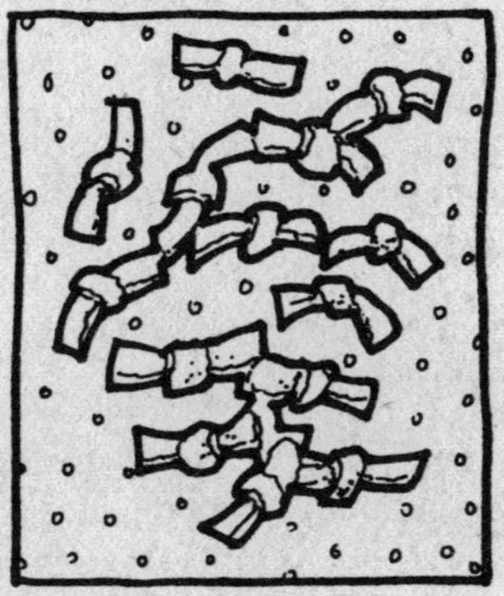

MACAROONS

Amaretti

Light, crisp almond biscuits that are often used as a decorative topping for desserts and cakes, or crushed to stuff apricots or sprinkle over ice cream.

Imperial (Metric)	**American**
4 oz (100g) blanched almonds	1 cupful blanched almonds
Pinch of salt	Pinch of salt
2 egg whites	2 egg whites
½ lb (225g) raw cane sugar, powdered in grinder	1 cupful raw cane sugar, powdered in grinder
Natural vanilla extract	Natural vanilla extract
½ teaspoonful finely grated lemon peel (optional)	½ teaspoonful finely grated lemon peel (optional)
Rice paper (optional)	Rice paper (optional)

1. Grind the almonds as fine as possible, then set aside.
2. Add the salt to the egg whites and beat until the mixture is frothy. Gradually add the sugar, still beating continually so that eventually the mixture is quite stiff.
3. Carefully fold in the ground almonds, a few drops of vanilla extract, and the lemon peel.
4. Arrange the rice paper in tins and drop the prepared mixture onto it in small mounds, leaving room for the *amaretti* to spread. (Alternatively, drop them onto greased, floured baking sheets.)
5. Bake at 350°F/180°C (Gas Mark 4) for 20 minutes, or until a light golden colour. Cool slightly, remove from the tins, and tear or cut around each one to remove the excess rice paper. Leave to get completely cold before storing in a tin.

HONEY NUT BISCUITS
Sospiri

Imperial (Metric)	**American**
10 oz (275g) self-raising wholemeal flour	2½ cupsful self-raising wholewheat flour
Pinch of bicarbonate of soda	Pinch of baking soda
Pinch of salt	Pinch of salt
4 oz (100g) margarine or butter	½ cupful margarine or butter
4 oz (100g) raw cane sugar	½ cupful raw cane sugar
5 oz (130g) honey	½ cupful honey
1 egg	1 egg
2 oz (50g) almonds, walnuts or roasted hazelnuts	½ cupful almonds, English walnuts or roasted hazelnuts

1. Sift together the flour, bicarbonate of soda and salt.
2. In a separate bowl cream together the margarine, sugar and honey. Beat the egg lightly and add to the mixture.
3. When well blended, combine this mixture with the dry ingredients, including the chopped nuts, and knead lightly.
4. Divide the dough into two, roll into logs approximately 2 in. (5cm) in diameter. Wrap in aluminium foil or clingfilm, and chill in the fridge for at least a few hours, preferably overnight.
5. Unwrap the logs and use a sharp knife to cut them into thin slices. Arrange these on lightly greased baking sheets and cook at 350°F/180°C (Gas Mark 4) for 10-15 minutes, or until the *sospiri* are golden. Cool on a wire rack, then store in a biscuit tin.

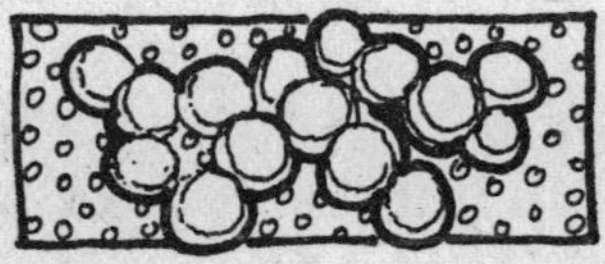

ITALIAN FRUIT BREAD

Panettone

Traditionally eaten at Christmas and Easter.

Imperial (Metric)	**American**
½ oz (12g) dried yeast	1 tablespoonful dried yeast
4 tablespoonsful warm milk	⅓ cupful warm milk
4 oz (100g) margarine or butter	½ cupful margarine or butter
1½ oz (40g) raw cane sugar	¼ cupful raw cane sugar
3 eggs	3 eggs
¾ lb (350g) plain wholemeal flour	3 cupsful plain wholewheat flour
Pinch of salt	Pinch of salt
2 oz (50g) raisins	¼ cupful raisins
2 oz (50g) candied peel	¼ cupful candied peel
Egg and water to glaze	Egg and water to glaze

1. Mix the yeast into the milk, and when it has dissolved, set aside to froth up.
2. Meanwhile, cream together the margarine and sugar. Beat the eggs and add them to the margarine.
3. Sift together the flour and salt. Stir in the yeast, then the second mixture, and knead gently for a few minutes to combine all the ingredients, so that you have a soft, smooth dough.
4. Flatten the dough slightly, sprinkle with half of the raisins and peel, then fold and knead again. Repeat this process so that all the fruits have been added to the dough, and are evenly distributed.
5. Put the dough in a warm bowl, cover, and leave in a warm, draught-free place for 1-2 hours, or until the dough has doubled in size.
6. Knead again lightly, then place the dough in a greased 8 in. (20cm) cake tin and put back in the same place. Leave it until it is well risen again.

7. Brush the top generously with a mixture of lightly beaten egg and water. Bake for 10 minutes at 400°F/200°C (Gas Mark 6), and then for a further 30-40 minutes at 350°F/180°C (Gas Mark 4).

8. When cooked, the *panettone* will be golden brown and firm to touch. Cool on a wire rack.

BREAD STICKS
Grissini

These can be served with soups or pâtés, put on the table instead of bread or eaten as a between-meal snack.

Imperial (Metric)	American
½ oz (12g) dried yeast	1 tablespoonful dried yeast
Approx. ⅓ pint (200ml) warm water	¾ cupful warm water
1 teaspoonful salt	1 teaspoonful salt
10 oz (275g) plain wholewheat flour	2½ cupsful plain wholemeal flour
Egg and milk to glaze	Egg and milk to glaze
Coarse sea salt	Coarse sea salt

1. Mix the yeast in a little of the warm water, and set aside.
2. Sift together the salt and flour, then stir in the bubbly yeast mixture and enough warm water to make a soft dough.
3. On a lightly floured board knead the dough for 5 minutes until smooth and pliable. Place it in a warmed bowl, cover, and leave in a warm place for 1-2 hours, or until doubled in size.
4. Knead briefly again, return the dough to the bowl and set aside in the warm to rise again.
5. Now use a rolling pin to gently flatten pieces of the dough into rectangles about ¼ in. (6mm) thick.
6. Use a floured knife to cut these into 1 in. (25mm) wide strips, and use your hands to roll them into pencil-like sticks.
7. Arrange these, leaving a little space between them, on greased baking sheets and brush with a drop of egg and milk, beaten together.
8. Leave in the warm for a further hour to double in size. Brush lightly with more egg and milk, and sprinkle with coarse sea salt.

9. Bake at 400°F/200°C (Gas Mark 6) for 15-20 minutes, or until the *grissini* are crisp. Cool on a wire rack and store in an airtight tin to use as needed.

Note: Although bread sticks are usually coated with salt in Italy, you can occasionally find them coated in sesame seeds, which gives them a completely different character. If the idea appeals to you, follow the above recipe exactly, but sprinkle the sticks with raw sesame seeds instead of salt before baking them.

APRICOT FLAN

Budino di albicocche

Imperial (Metric)	**American**
½ lb (225g) plain wholemeal flour	2 cupsful plain wholewheat flour
4 oz (100g) margarine or butter	½ cupful margarine or butter
4 oz (100g) vanilla sugar*	½ cupful vanilla sugar*
2 small egg yolks	2 small egg yolks
Water to mix	Water to mix
1½ lb (¾ kilo) fresh apricots	1½ pounds fresh apricots
2 oz (50g) raw cane sugar	¼ cupful raw cane sugar
2 oz (50g) flaked almonds	½ cupful slivered almonds

1. Sift the flour into a bowl, then rub in the margarine to make a mixture that resembles fine breadcrumbs.
2. Stir in the sugar, the lightly beaten egg yolks, and just enough cold water to make a fairly firm dough. Knead briefly, then wrap in aluminium foil or clingfilm, and chill for at least 30 minutes.
3. Meanwhile, halve and stone the apricots. Wash them, then poach in the minimum amount of water, plus the sugar, for 10-20 minutes, or until they are just beginning to soften, but still hold their shape.
4. Roll out the dough and use it to line a 9 in. (23cm) flan dish (or use a smaller dish, and reserve some of the dough to make a decorative lattice pattern over the top).
5. Drain the apricots and arrange them cut side down, in rings over the base of the flan. Sprinkle with the nuts.
6. Bake for 10 minutes at 400°F/200°C (Gas Mark 6), then for 10-15 minutes more at 375°F/190°C (Gas Mark 5), or until the pastry is cooked. Leave to cool before serving.

*Vanilla sugar can be made by adding vanilla pods to sugar which is then stored in a jar until the sugar absorbs the flavour.

INDEX